Fulfilled Kids
Fulfilled Parents

How to reach your children's hearts through their heads

BY RICK DOUGHTY

First Printing 2011

LCCN: 2011940608
ISBN-10: 1937285006
ISBN-13: 978-1937285005

FTF Press
Beaverton, OR 97006

www.ftfpress.com

Acknowledgments

To Sally: You are a lovely woman, a wonderful mentor, and a great friend. I cannot thank you enough for taking my hand and joining me on this parenting journey.

To Grahm, Heather, and Hannah: You three are what this book is all about. Thank you for being regular kids with open hearts to your regular parents.

To Rich Allen and Eric Jensen: You caught my attention and interested me in the brain. Thank you for making neuroscience understandable, useful, and even entertaining.

To my editor, Jodi Tahsler, and all those who spent their valuable time reading manuscripts of the book and providing encouragement and feedback: Shelley Gunton, Ted Hobbs, Denise Urbanski, Brian Horne, Jennifer Visser, and Sue Templeton. Thank you for reading with great care and insight. Your comments and corrections were incredibly helpful.

Finally to Jim Newby and all those who encouraged me to put my seminars into a book form, thank you!

Foreword

When my wife and I began parenting, we read a number of parenting books because we wanted to do a good job. Those books were wonderful and very helpful; however, there seemed to be something missing. Our continuing search brought us to consider what scientists were figuring out about how our kids' brains worked.

As we pursued this knowledge, it made sense to us that a good book about this would be extremely helpful. There have been times we have had to know how to deal with anger, or pimples, or dating, or breast feeding, or a specific age range, and we are genuinely thankful for all the information that people have written on those topics. However, a parent deals with most of these only at certain times.

One thing we found that we had to deal with every day throughout parenting was what was going on in our kids' heads. From their brain came their behavior and the way in which they interacted with us. A good understanding of how their brains developed and worked seemed like it would be incredibly helpful to us. We found it was!

It transformed our parenting and has given us three college-age students who are very thankful for the way we parented. In a sense, we reached their hearts through their heads. We would contend that, if you only have time for one parenting book, this is it! What I have included in this book is the information that was most helpful to my wife and me. We sincerely hope that you find this information as helpful as we did.

I need to note that all the names in this book are fictitious and do not represent anyone I know.

Table of Contents

Chapter 1

Parenting and Brains

When my kids were in grade school, I began attending seminars on brain development. The organizers of these seminars believed that learning how the brain worked would help us educate kids more effectively. That made sense to me. I had stayed awake long enough in basic biology to understand that the brain was central to learning and behavior. I jumped into these learning opportunities with both feet and found that not only did they help with education, but they also helped with parenting. My most memorable application of brain development to parenting took place one spring night about 10 pm. At that time, I had two kids in middle school and one in grade school. My wife had just gotten a phone call, and she related that some out-of-town friends were planning to join us the following evening for dinner. We were having an unusual stretch of nice weather and decided to eat outside.

I walked over to the patio door, accompanied by our dog Hunter, and flipped on the backyard light. Hunter's diligent work over the winter showed up everywhere. In our family, it is the kids' job to take care of pets, and one of those jobs is picking up the dog poop. Oregon winters are usually rainy, and the job does not get done as regularly as it should. I would have been happy with the job being done occasionally during the winter, but at this point it looked like nothing had been picked up for months. I had several options.

A. Go on a rant! Outrage and disbelief at the wanton disregard for our mutually agreed upon chores were poised and ready to strike. It was after 10 pm, and I was upset that we had to deal with this late at night. I anticipated a fight, but since I was the biggest, that dog poop would get picked up!

B. Go on a rant, but only internally. Then be reasonably nice but firmly directive with the kids. If I kept the tone light, maybe the level of conflict would be minimal. Even with a diplomatic approach, we would still have to figure out whose turn it was. This would begin with three fingers pointed in different directions as each would remember why he or she did it last, and why it was someone else's turn. One predictable outcome would be the older two would remember that it was the youngest one's turn. This might go better than option A, but I suspected it would still be fraught with difficulties.

C. It occurred to me I could try a brain friendly option. *Hmmm*, I thought, *I have nothing to lose, except a yard still filled with dog poop, and a quick clean-up by everyone tomorrow afternoon.* Okay, I decided, let's jump off the brain development bridge, give it a try, and see what happens.

I walked upstairs to find three children in various stages of late-night vegetation. I got their attention and announced, "The dog poop needs to be picked up, and one of you has won the dog poop lottery. The results will be at the breakfast table tomorrow morning!" I then went downstairs and put three names in a hat. I pulled the names out one by one, beginning with the winner and ending with the loser (depending on your perspective, of course). I put a note on the winner's chair that said, "You won the dog poop lottery! Please pick up the dog poop from the back yard as we have guests coming over for dinner." I left notes scheduling future poop pickups for the runner up and the loser and went to bed.

The next morning, both my wife and I were up and out the door before our esteemed winner woke up. The last thing I thought before leaving was, *There's no way this will work.* When I got home late that afternoon, I walked straight to the back yard to find… all the dog poop had been picked up. I stood in amazement and reflected on this for a moment. Wow! A middle school child had completed an unpopular chore without conflict or complaining. This seemed like proof for the existence of an alternate reality. Maybe the middle school years could be different than what was commonly experienced!

The strategy I had just implemented was from a lesson in building better relationships through State Management that Eric Jensen had taught me in his brain-based learning workshops, and that I read about later in his book *Tools for Engagement*.[1] I began to intentionally use State Management at home, as well as in my work in classrooms. State Management takes into account the temporary disposition or mental state a child is in, and intentionally uses transitions to minimize conflict when making a request (more on this in chapter five). It was not magic, but over time, it made an incredibly positive difference in the behavior of kids and in my relationship to them. If that was the only thing I learned from the scientists and communicators who taught about brain development, it would have been enough, but there's more!

I learned that many of the things I had been taught about the brain when I was growing up were not entirely true. Here are some wrong lessons that I remember. Maybe you remember these as well.

- Wrong lesson #1 – We get our lifetime supply of brain cells by the time we're six, and we don't produce any more. We spend the rest of our life killing them off through various activities, such as drinking too much alcohol on Friday night. In the 60's and 70's, this belief lead to careful consideration by many college students as to how many brain cells were needed to pass the coming exam versus how many brain cells could be expended to have weekend fun. This understanding of no new brain cells is flat-out wrong. We generate new brain cells throughout our entire life. Now, please don't misunderstand my point. I am not promoting killing more brain cells on Friday night, because we make new ones on Saturday. But this does make us think in new ways about the brain.
- Wrong lesson #2 – At the age of six, your brain was the size of an adult brain and was done developing. What happened from

age six on was that you simply trained the adult brain to act like an adult. My childhood experience made me think this training could take anywhere from six to sixty years. Gary, quarterback of my middle school football team, was six feet tall and hairy when he was twelve years old and seemed to me in every way to be an adult. Then there was my uncle who, at sixty-six, had apparently missed his adult training and still acted like a kid. So it seemed what the scientists were saying about the six-year-old brain was correct. Wrong again. The six-year-old brain, though approaching the size of an adult brain, is extremely underdeveloped in certain ways and won't be an adult brain in terms of complete development until about age twenty-five. Do you know what age car insurance rates drop? Twenty-five! The insurance companies have known this for years, long before the neuroscientists. They knew people made better decisions and were better drivers at age twenty-five. They just didn't know why. Now we know. At twenty-five (approximately) our brains are finally fully developed. This has huge implications for parenting. No matter how mature children appear, parents can't expect to be dealing with a fully mature adult brain until the mid-twenties.

- Wrong lesson #3 – Children all go crazy around the age of thirteen because of hormones. Hormones are all over the map at this time of life, and since you can't reason with hormones, you just write off any hope of significant progress in kids for a number of years. In fact, one of the pop theories in the 80's was so extreme on this point, that it almost sounded like we should lock our children in a room for three years, push food under the door, hope they survived, and let them out when they were sixteen or older. Wrong, wrong, wrong. Yes, hormones definitely take off at this time of life, but even more important for parents is that huge changes are taking place in the brain—changes that weren't even suspected when I was a kid. How parents approach this time of their child's life is greatly affected by what they understand to be happening.

I could go on, but you get the idea. These wrong ideas that originated with scientists have all been corrected by scientists. This should give us a sense of caution. Neuroscience can provide tremendous help, but it can also misinform, and it certainly doesn't have all the answers. Our task is to take what seem to be solid findings of neuroscience and use them to help our parenting efforts become more effective. Most of us have learned some tricks and tips about parenting that work, starting with the way we were raised. We need to take the best of what we have found works in parenting and combine it with the findings of neuroscience.

In my own experience, there were some incredibly insightful people who helped me through the challenges of growing up. They weren't neuroscientists, and they didn't give too much thought to these wrong ideas. They had wisdom about kids that seemed to come from experience passed down from generation to generation. They did a great job with raising kids whether the kid was four, fourteen, or twenty-four. We've all known parents like this.

Where did these parents get their knowledge before neuroscientists were around? They were students of life and behavior and not only learned from their own experience but also from others with wise advice. So what does it mean when a neuroscientist tells you that the brain isn't fully developed until age twenty-five? In the case of the insurance companies, they say, "Thanks for filling in the details, but we essentially already knew that." As a wise parent, you can agree that the information is interesting and then continue your great parenting, made more knowledgeable because of the neuroscientists' work.

My point is that learning more about how the brain functions is not the magical answer to every parenting problem, and neuroscientists have already taught us by the misinformation of the sixties that not everything they say is correct. Fortunately, the good neuroscientists insist that others confirm their findings before they share their knowledge with us. I have found learning how the brain works incredibly helpful. Some of you may find that what I write in this book may simply be confirmation of the good parenting practices you already have. That would please me to no end. My hope is that others will read what I write, be encouraged, and find new ideas.

Please keep the following in mind as you read: to the best of my knowledge, the information in this book is up-to-date with current research, and I am presenting the ideas from neuroscience that have been the most helpful to my wife and me in our parenting. The reality is that I may have missed some important ideas, and may have included some not-so-important ideas. In the end, you and I have the same task. We need to consider these ideas and then decide for ourselves and our families the healthiest and wisest ways to parent.

Chapter 2

Filler	Follower	Finder	Fulfiller
0..........2.....................11..................18...............25			

From Filler to Fulfiller

The brain goes through some incredible times of growth. During the development of a fetus, the brain produces up to 250,000 neurons (brain cells) a minute. Both producing neurons and getting rid of unneeded neurons continues at an incredible pace until about age two. Sometime after that, the pace slows. Brain development continues at a relatively stable rate until the age of eleven or twelve. Around this time, there is another explosive change, and the brain overproduces potential neural (brain cell) connections. It then gets rid of, or prunes, the connections that aren't used. These connections are an important part of the wiring of our brain, and just like a lot of extra fishing line can get tangled up in a big knot, so all these extra connections can create a mess. In some ways, that's not a bad description for a teenager's brain.

Just like it takes time to untangle fishing line knots, it takes time for a teenage brain to organize itself. A huge reconstruction of the brain will take place through the teen years, slowing down as kids grow into their twenties. At this time brain development becomes more stable and finishes somewhere around age twenty-five.

Besides these general time periods in brain development, it is important for parents to understand one other significant aspect of development. Areas of the brain come "online" at different times throughout these twenty-five years of brain development. What I call coming online, scientists call *myelination*. Myelination is a biological process by which the neurons in the brain become more efficient at transmitting their bits of information. Although a significant portion of the brain is in place by age six, many of its parts have not been myelinated or come online yet. This means that although they exist, they don't work very well. Knowing when areas of the brain come online is helpful in understanding how the brain works and how we should parent. For our purposes in this book, we will refer to this myelination process as coming online. One common misunderstanding that may result from using the term *online* is the idea that if a brain area isn't *online* then it doesn't work. The truth is that as long as the brain area has developed, it will work even before it goes online, but it will be slower and simply not work as well.

This simple and short description of brain development and areas coming online forms the basis for what I refer to as Filler to Fulfiller (FTF) Parenting. Based on brain development, I divide the parenting job into four stages. The first is the Filler stage, which roughly corresponds with that first explosion of brain development and lasts until about age two. The next is that Follower stage, a relatively stable period of robust brain growth, which lasts from approximately age three until age eleven. The Finder stage, a period of key changes affecting behavior, is roughly from ages twelve until age eighteen. The Fulfiller stage of brain development lasts from about age nineteen to about age twenty-five.

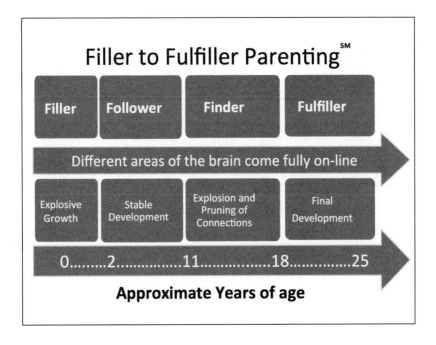

Did you notice I used the words *approximately, roughly,* and *about?* What this means is that these age ranges can vary for any particular child. We can't say, "Our son turned twelve, and now he is a Finder." However, if we are familiar with the Finder characteristics, trust me, we will recognize it when it happens.

I still remember the day when I realized my son had become a Finder. He probably didn't change overnight, but it certainly seemed like it. One day, my wife and I had what seemed to be a very sensible, straightforward grade-schooler, and the next day we had a confused middle-schooler. Here's what happened.

The sun was shining, and my son and I were standing on our back deck. I was explaining something to my son, and he couldn't get it. The more I tried, the less he seemed to understand. I was looking into the blank face of a talented and intelligent son who would have understood what I was saying only six months earlier. What was even more confusing, he would have understood this very well in fifth grade, years earlier. Starting my third attempt at explanation, I was beginning to get frustrated. I was using illustrations, arm motions, carefully chosen words, and wondering if I needed visual aids and an interpreter.

This confusion might be on purpose, I thought, *He might be intentionally ignoring me. He knows what I am saying. Why is he acting like this?*

Then it dawned on me. "This is it," that little voice in my head exclaimed. "This is when their brains get foggy. This is what the neuroscientists predicted would happen." I remember stopping mid-sentence and heading inside, excited to see what I had been learning happening right before my eyes and wanting to immediately tell my wife. I ran inside the house to proclaim to her, "The fog has come!"

True to the neuroscientists' prediction, the clear minded, sensible grade-schooler was gone. A wonderful change had started, and in significant ways, my job as a parent also changed. It took a bit of time for my wife and I to adjust, but learning about and preparing for this change was a tremendous help both to us as parents and to our son.

That is what this book is about. It is getting us as parents prepared for significant changes in our kids' brains and learning how these affect our parenting. If we know the characteristics of these changes, we will recognize them when they come. This information was and continues to be a great help to my wife and me, and our hope is that it will be a great help to you as well. To get started, we are going to quickly overview the entire FTF Parenting approach in this chapter; then we will discuss each segment in depth in the following chapters.

The Filler Stage (approximately 0 to 2 years)

For our consideration of how to parent, this stage of brain development takes place from shortly after conception until about age two. This time, as I mentioned earlier, is marked by the birth of huge numbers of neurons. The brain actually produces more neurons than it needs and then removes excess or unused neurons.

To understand the characteristics of this stage, we will consider the process by which a child learns to talk. If you have an infant, you know that they love to imitate you. If you stick out your tongue, they stick out their tongue. If you make noises with your mouth, they try to make noises with their mouth. Why is this? It is almost as if, when the doctor or nurse whisked them away right after birth to weigh them and check their general health, they were given a pep talk about the need to imitate mom and dad.

Of course, we know they didn't get that pep talk, but parts of their brain develop and come online that cause them to try and imitate the behaviors that they see and hear. This is not a conscious decision. Our kids are instinctually driven to do it. At the center of this imitating activity are special brain cells called mirror neurons. As soon as babies can get control of their little bodies and orient themselves toward something interesting (like your face) they will begin focusing and imitating.

This is a good example of what is called implicit learning. The infant is not conscious of the fact that they are learning from imitating. The brain is simply downloading all kinds of information from the environment. That's why I call this "the Filler stage," because that is primarily what is going on. The brain is filling itself with information by downloading it as quickly as it can, primarily directed by the areas of the brain that are coming online.

Learning to speak a language is a great example of this. The desire to imitate things like facial expressions begins early. Then around six to twelve months, a part of the brain comes online that begins analyzing what sounds are being heard. At this point, the brain automatically identifies and records the basic sounds of any language being spoken to them by their parents and caregivers.

By the first year, kids' brains are wired to hear or produce all the sounds in the languages they've been hearing during that year. Along with this, the parts of the brain that are able to understand language come online, and a little later, the parts that are able to produce language come online. All of a sudden, without a Rosetta Stone course or any time spent in the classroom, they begin to speak English or Spanish or maybe both. This is a great example of a process I like to call the "my brain made me do it" process. This is a characteristic that will stick with your children to one extent or another throughout their development. In the Filler stage, children have no conscious idea they are learning a language, and yet it happens whether anyone likes it or not.

One really cool story about this built-in language ability came from a group of deaf children in Nicaragua.[2] They were placed into a school where the teachers lacked the knowledge and ability to teach sign language. This did not hinder them. Over time the children developed a new sign language among themselves. Isn't that wild? Without ever intending to, designing, forming committees, or hiring a linguist, these children invented a new language. This is largely implicit learning. Our children are going to be driven to download whatever is around them and attempt to put that learning to use.

Language is a great example of the Filler stage and implicit learning. No tutors, no classes, no commitments, no motivational speakers—the learning just happens, and it happens to all kinds of kids with all kinds of IQ's in all kinds of languages all around the world. What does this mean for our parenting? I will explore the implications in the Filler Chapter.

The Follower Stage (approximately 3 to 11 years)

In the Follower stage, roughly from age three to eleven, this implicit learning continues. As we move through the stages, keep in mind that the next stage almost always includes the characteristics of the previous stage. However, changes are taking place and new

capabilities are being added. These changes cause each stage to
differ, and affect our parenting approach as well. Toward the end of
the Filler stage and into the Follower stage children will begin to
think about learning, will cooperate (or at times not cooperate) in
learning, and will begin to be intentional to one extent or another
about things they want to learn. These changes add explicit
learning (learning that is intentional and can be described by the
child) to implicit learning.

This stage is extra fun! You can see the wheels turning in your
kids' heads as they work to put things together. For instance, we
were picking raspberries at Grandpa's and Grandma's house and
one of us passed gas. Our oldest was about three years old, and he
immediately said in his cute, childish voice, "Uh-oh, dropped a
raspberry." He was putting together how dropped things made
noises. We got a good laugh out of this, and have had many other
good laughs seeing how kids begin to express their thoughts.

This age then presents a wonderful opportunity that is
appropriately called the Follower stage. Children are learning like
crazy and wanting to follow someone to learn from. Implicit learning
is still taking place, and their mirror neurons are as active as ever.
Added to this, they begin to recognize that they are learning and
cooperate consciously with that learning. This is explicit learning,
and at this stage, we have an incredible ability to influence our kids'
learning. The great parenting opportunity at this stage is passing
on our knowledge as well as values, habits, and commitments. They
will learn both from what we do and what we teach.

I remember being out on the playground in third grade. Two of
my friends got into an argument that turned into a classic fist fight

(to the delight of many of us). They were swinging, grappling, and rolling on the ground, surrounded by a knot of screaming spectators until the duty teacher showed up. It was everything a third grade boy dreams of in a good fight. Why were they fighting? The argument began as to whether Richard Nixon (Republican) or Hubert Humphrey (Democrat) would win the coming election. Their nine-year-old heated words soon turned to flying fists and rolling bodies, over being a Democrat or Republican?!

Did these friends of mine really understand conservatism versus liberalism? Did they feel that civil rights issues could be settled through education and tax incentives? Did they differ over policy toward the war in Vietnam or the War on Poverty? You and I know they had no idea about this stuff. Why were they fighting? They fought because their parents were Democrats or Republicans. They were willing to go to the mat for what mom and dad believed. Wow!

This is the tremendous opportunity of the Follower stage. If we are present and involved in our kids' lives, they will pick up our knowledge and values. A danger also exists. They are looking to follow someone. If we aren't there, they will follow someone else; maybe someone they shouldn't follow. That can create problems. How should this affect our parenting? Stay tuned for the Follower chapter.

The Finder Stage (approximately 12 to 18 years)

If at first glance the Follower stage is extra fun, the Finder stage is extra unnerving. For a devoted parent, most of the time the Follower stage will lull you into this fun little dream world in which your child becomes a responsible, amazingly mature, thoughtful democratic social reformer who respects the environment. Guess who else is a democratic social reformer with respect for the environment—you! You will be tempted at this stage with your first child to look at the parents of middle school maniacs and wonder where these parents went wrong. What did they do in the parenting process to produce this mixed-up, back-talking, sloppy human being? There is an easy answer to this question: *wait.* That's correct. Just wait a few years, and chances are the answer will come roaring into your life.

I need to add that the intensity of the answer will vary from child to child. There are kids who have a naturally more compliant temperament, and kids who have a naturally more defiant temperament. Wise parenting will also have an effect, but for kids to become capable adults, all have to follow the developmental process that comes in the Finder years. This stage should bring significant changes. I would be more worried if it did not.

As we have noted in the Follower years, brain growth is relatively stable from about three years until eleven years old or so. Changes and robust growth are taking place, but these changes are of a different nature than the changes that will happen around the age of twelve or thirteen. Around this time, there is an explosion of potential neural connections in your kids' heads, making their thinking somewhat foggy and slow. Then, certain parts of the brain come online that tend to make them want to take risks and become oppositional. All of a sudden, your stable, wonderful child's brain begins to undergo major reconstruction, and they will never be the same again. And you shouldn't want them to be.

There is a noticeable change in the way in which kids think during this stage. I will refer to this change as "Teen Think" in this book. I haven't seen this term used much, but it helps me to have a way to specifically refer to the brain changes that take place around the age of twelve or thirteen, and it helps identify those changes without referring to the larger context of puberty. Puberty is a very important topic that I will only mention briefly in this book. I think we are going to find out more and more that there are a number of major changes taking place in kids' lives around this time, and they are likely dependent on each other.

If we go back a century, we find puberty taking place closer to age 16 or 17. Over the past hundred years, that age has come down significantly. Scientists don't agree on the reason for this change. It could be a combination of a number of factors—better nutrition; more light exposure from artificial light; chemicals in our diet that mimic sex hormones. A likely reality is that changes in our modern society are shortening childhood from a biological standpoint, and this has implications for parenting. No matter what scientists find, I think it is useful to have a term, Teen Think, referring to the brain changes taking place around twelve or thirteen and to identify those specific brain changes without reference to all the changes of puberty.

These brain changes seem to have at least the following effects. Kids lose some clarity and speed in their thinking process. They tend to become more oppositional and want to take more risks. They have a heightened emotional/social component to their thinking, and that thinking tends to be black and white; things are either right or wrong. Science will help us understand more in the future what Teen Think is. I am convinced it is real, it is good, and it is based on developmental changes that take place in the brain right around the beginning of the teenage years.

Before the teenage years, a lot of our kids are just little replicas of us in many ways. This is a wonderful thing, but this doesn't prepare them or motivate them sufficiently to go out into life and make all of the changes they need to make to become adults. To become an adult, they need to leave their parents and identify with their own age group (this is a good thing that will get them out on their own someday). They need to want to be different from their parents and have their own opinions (this is also a good thing, as they must become their own person). Finally they need to want to make some risky decisions (this is also very good, and I'll explain why in more detail in the Finder chapter). Much of this is a result of changes in the brain over which they have no control. These changes make them think like teens.

Basically, they are finding out who they are apart from us as parents. These changes are probably similar to what drives a bird to leave the nest, or male monkeys to leave their troop and join a new one. It's likely not a conscious decision on these animals' parts. It is one outgrowth of the "my brain made me do it" principle.

Changes take place in our kids' brains that drive them to want to explore, discover, take risks, and leave childhood to become adults. To do this, just as birds or monkeys do, our kids have to leave home. Also, in the same way as birds or monkeys, our kids don't make a conscious decision at age twelve to pencil in "move out of the house" on their schedules. Rather, changes in their brains take place that begin to drive them to leave childhood and become adults. This is a really good and valuable thing, but it can be incredibly traumatic if we don't understand it. Most parents and children are unprepared for this change.

This is where we have a great advantage over birds and monkeys. We can talk to our kids for years before this change happens and prepare them. While they are Followers and listening, we can prepare our minds and their hearts for the fact that Teen Think will come, and although it will cause some friction, it is a fantastic thing. No one publishes the arrival schedule for our particular child, but usually like a freight train that can't be ignored, Teen Think arrives.

One day, it seems, an alien comes to inhabit our child's brain, and we freak out. Where did my sweet little Samantha go? Why is she hanging around friends like that, piercing her body, and not wanting to be seen with me? Why does she try to kill her little brother on a daily basis (death by insult)? Who taught her to roll her eyes and grunt like that...do they have a secret middle school class on all this stuff?

As parents, we think our children are perfectly aware of what they are doing and how they are behaving, and we are incensed! This behavior seems premeditated and intentional, and we want to sit our kids down and set them straight. For many of us who try this approach, our efforts can go horribly wrong with the former child, now young adult, running out of the room sobbing, "You don't understand," or screaming something worse. Well, there's news to come about this typical parent-child interaction in the Finder chapter. This is a fantastic time of life, but it helps to know what is changing in their brains so that we cooperate with and facilitate those changes rather than oppose them.

The Fulfiller Stage (approximately 19 to 25 years)

The teenage years don't last forever; they just seem like they do. Honestly, apart from a couple of rocky years of children acting like their siblings were the worst things on earth, and a year of my wife and I fighting over how we were going to respond to these changes, we really did enjoy these years. This stage was different than the Follower years, but it was an exhilarating challenge that involved us in the growth of our children into adults. The Finder years (teenage years) have been exciting years for my wife and me as parents. If these years are navigated with understanding, they go reasonably well, and the basis is laid for a productive, cooperative, lifetime relationship with our young adults that often begins in the Fulfiller stage.

In the Fulfiller stage, brain reconstruction begins to slow down. The brain is still under development that will continue until their mid-twenties. One of the most distinct characteristics of this time of development is that the final brain systems come fully online, like the frontal cortex, and these changes make the brain able to function in more complex ways.

In the Finder years, the brain increases in its ability to consider abstract concepts, such as math or love. The Fulfiller brain will continue this developmental process and become better able to consider multiple abstractions at the same time, helping it to better understand calculus or relationships. The Fulfiller also increases in their ability to think ahead, problem-solve, prioritize, and control their emotions. Increases in abilities like these give birth to full adult capabilities.

This is the stage in which our kids normally take all they've downloaded, all we've taught, all they've learned about themselves, and all their energy for independence and apply these to their own lives, taking risks for themselves and heading out on their own to pursue their goals and dreams. This is why I refer to this stage as the Fulfiller stage. We are learning this can be done in such a way that our kids see us as partners with them in their pursuits.

Our story of the Fulfiller stage is still being developed as I write this book. So far it has gone well. We have three college-age kids, and as we explore this stage together in this book, you will find me as much a learner now as I have tried to be at each prior stage. At this stage, as any other, l lean on others' experiences and learning, along with neuroscience for help.

One aspect I can't emphasize enough from a brain developmental standpoint is that, even though the changes in the teenage years have begun to level out, our kids' brains are not fully developed until the mid-twenties (and even after that brains change throughout our lives). We continually encourage our kids in the Fulfiller stage to think about their plans, to write out the pros and cons, to consider how decisions have gone, and to be creative and try things. In other words, we are still working to encourage them in good brain health habits while letting them know they're in charge of their lives. They will benefit from their good choices and struggle with their bad choices. We have officially set them free to determine their own lives.

Getting Ready to Parent!

These stages and their characteristics will vary from child to child in their timing and extent, but all children go through this general developmental pathway. There are numerous factors that will affect development in each of our children, and clear examples of these differences can be seen in males versus females.

Early on, females are hard wired to be more attentive to faces than males. So when I talk about attunement or kids getting in sync with our attitudes, expressions, and feelings in the Filler stage, girls will generally do this better than boys. If we notice that our little girls love to look at our faces and our little boys look and then seem to get bored and look elsewhere, we need to know that there is nothing wrong with either of them. Their gender has a definite effect on the extent of this characteristic.

In the same way, in the Finder stage, I will mention that girls and boys will differ in their emotional maturation rate. Not only that, but because levels of the female hormones are varying widely in adolescent girls, whereas testosterone levels always seem high in adolescent boys, emotional swings will tend to be more pronounced in girls than boys. Both sexes, however, go through a similar brain maturation process in the emotional areas.

There isn't enough room in this book to handle all of these influences and variation; however, if we understand the general developmental pathway, we will be much better prepared as parents to recognize it in each of our kids and work with it. This will help to minimize the frustration and fears that come from not understanding what is happening.

This is important, because frustrations and fears can get in the way of successful parenting. For my wife and me, it seemed these varied throughout the parenting process, and certain fears can be paralyzing to good parenting and potentially damage our relationships, either our relationship to our kids or our relationship to our spouse. To me, love and fear are opponents. One cannot exist robustly in the presence of the other. Love helps eject fear and frustration from our homes, or fear and frustration can eject love. Our homes and lives should be crammed full of love, not fear and frustration, and from time to time it will be worth our while in this book to face some common fears and frustrations and discuss them.

I will start the next chapter with the assumption that you have kids, or that you or your significant other is pregnant, and parenting is a certainty for you. Before I make that assumption, it may be helpful to consider that there are a number of us who had really terrible or traumatic childhoods and fear doing to our kids what was done to us. One very effective way to avoid this is to not have kids. I can't say if that is the best decision for you. However, one thing I do know for sure is that the decision should not be made on the basis of fear.

Fear motivates us to move quickly in a safe direction. But those fears should not be the ultimate decision maker and should always be reflected on and analyzed at some point. My dad provided an excellent example of how to handle fear.

I learned from him that when a dog is making a beeline for you, fangs bared and barking wickedly, fear is a very appropriate response. It heightens our senses and mobilizes our energy. However, to let fear control what we do would be a disaster. Fear would normally dictate that we turn and run, and that action would ensure we would be taken down by the dog. Fear sets the stage, but we still have to make a decision based on the best information available and good thinking.

My dad was attacked by dogs more than once in his life. Dogs trained to attack. He almost always stood his ground. Because my dad had trained hunting dogs as a kid, he was asked to begin his military career as an officer in the Canine Corps during World War II. He became a "teaser" who aided in training attack dogs in the Army. He wore protective equipment and goaded the dogs while they were being controlled and trained by their handlers.

His first attack by a dog was in the military. After one tease session, a dog broke off the tease line and headed full speed for my dad, who had already taken off his protective equipment. Dad stood his ground and cuffed the dog boxing style on the side of the head repeatedly until the dog's handler showed up. Another time, when he was in his eighties, he stood his ground as well, raised his walking stick and, as the dog leapt off the ground for him, he cuffed the dog across the side of the head with the stick, turning him around in midair, and sending him running home with his tail between his legs.

Did my dad ever run from an attacking dog? Absolutely. I was on his shoulders one time. He was ten feet from an open door, and he made it inside and shut the door before the snarling dog could reach him. This time, it was a good decision for him not to stand his ground. Did he feel fear? I am certain he did. However, even this decision to run was not based on fear, but on quick thinking about the options that were available to him. Was there fear in him in all these situations? Of course. The fear energized him, but it did not decide for him.

If having children sounds like the wrong thing for you, I invite you to keep reading. I think this book will help you evaluate if your decision is based on good reason or fear.

Great information and encouragement await us as we explore the Filler, Follower, Finder, and Fulfiller stages. I've always enjoyed a treasure hunt, and in many ways, the parental journey is like a treasure hunt. There is tremendous potential for goodness, courage, love, accomplishment, and humor in our kids. One of the opportunities of parenting is to explore with our kids their particular characteristics and help them pursue their potential through their own developmental process.

I should comment now and likely will again later, that I am not dealing with things that go wrong with development in this book. Fortunately, there are excellent resources and help available for developmental deficits. In this book, we are going to focus on cooperating with the usual brain development taking place in our kids.

Chapter 3

Filler	Follower	Finder	Fulfiller

0..........2.....................11...................18...............25

Filler

Congratulations! You (or your wife) are pregnant. All of a sudden it strikes you: you're going to be a parent. I was the guy in this process, which meant I was naturally less connected to all that was going on. My wife was, understandably, closest to the situation, but we were both excited. Our first child was "nipponsei" (made in Japan). My wife got pregnant while we were living overseas. We like to say our oldest was made in Japan with American parts and labor and exported to the US.

We were living in Kobe, Japan, far away from family and friends, which brought certain advantages. We were establishing our lives and family independently, largely without social expectations of what others thought we should be. In other ways it brought disadvantages: we were a long way from family and friends for support and help. Fortunately, we had a great group of supportive friends in that country.

There were some clear advantages to living in Japan during our first pregnancy. It was pretty tough in the 80's to eat a lousy diet and get out of shape in Japan. We walked almost everywhere we went with an intervening train ride if necessary. We had access to a car, but finding a parking spot on the other end of most trips was almost impossible. In fact, you could not even buy a car in Kobe unless you had an official, registered parking spot. Most people walked to the market to go shopping every day. The veggies were fresh, fruits were fresh, fish was fresh, and exercise by walking was pervasive. Processed and fast foods were available, but they were expensive and not nearly as abundant as in the US.

These circumstances were perfect for the developing human being in my wife's body. The first things we begin filling in the **Filler** stage are the nutritional building blocks of life, and these are largely dependent on what mom eats. I remember heading out in Japan for a dinner composed of what Sumo wrestlers ate. If you are not familiar with Sumo, it is a sport that to a Westerner consists of two massively huge, obese-looking guys (often 300-plus pounds), dressed in nothing but fancy jock straps, who take less than 10 seconds to throw one another out of a circle. This happens after a lot of fanfare in which they stomp around, clap their hands, and throw what looks like chalk dust in the air. The one left in the circle wins.

What they eat is called *Chanko-nabe*. It is basically "whatever stew." You take whatever veggies and meat are around and stew them up in gargantuan proportions and consume. The thing I never understood was how they got so big on this diet. Admittedly the quantity was huge, and I was stuffed after eating my first *Chanko-nabe*. However, the main ingredients were water and veggies, and I was starving two hours after eating. I learned that the missing ingredient to the weight gain was a nice long nap on this full stomach.

Apart from Sumo wrestlers, the diet and lifestyle in Japan kept the rest of us trim and fit without jogging, vitamins, endless books about the latest lose-it-quick diet, or special factory-created bars that supposedly give us great nutrition. We simply ate non-processed fresh food and walked a lot. In fact, speaking of brain health, there is evidence that the countries with the lowest levels of depression are countries like Japan where large quantities of fresh fish are consumed.[3] Trust me, the fish was fresh in Japan. It took me a while to get used to buying my fish in the market while it was still flopping around.

In America, a good diet is a tough thing to find. We tend to fill our bodies with products of factories, not direct products of nature. We love to get our "natural" food in a can or bottle that says it's natural. There is a movement toward natural foods, but the factory is still in the middle of the process. The factory is working to convince us that "natural" can be had after processing. Some factories do a better job than others, but to be natural, the food should be processed as little as possible. Often, the more natural a food is, the less perfect it looks, and the more easily it spoils; meaning the food has a short shelf life. A short shelf life is a problem for factory food, because they need their products to be able to sit in warehouses, and then to sit on store shelves for a while in order to help them make their money.

Essentially a short shelf life is directly related to how nutritious the food is. The reason food goes bad is because small living organisms love it and thrive on it. Anytime shelf life is extended through a factory process, the food becomes less nutritious and sometimes actually toxic to those little living organisms. The problem is that our bodies are composed of little living organisms called cells, and if the food has a long shelf life, making it tough for a small living organism to thrive on, it's tougher for your cells and your body to thrive on. Also we have expectations that our food look good. So-called natural items may be picked early and artificially ripened, dyed, or covered with not-so-healthy stuff to make them shiny or colorful, or covered with pesticides to kill unwanted living things.

All of these factors, while having some understandable goals, make our food less nutritious, and some would argue even dangerous in certain ways. The main point to understand is that fresh and natural is healthy, and that in general the more processed a food is, the less healthy it becomes. Please note my phrase "in general." Some processing may be necessary for safety or for making a food useable, such as the milling of wheat. The point to keep in mind is that usually the less processing that takes place, the healthier the food is.

Japan, then, gave us a leg up on FTF Parenting and great brain development. It gave us a healthy diet of fresh natural veggies, fruits, and fish that included very little factory processed food. This great nutritional start was not because of our wise planning; we had no choice. Processed food was really expensive, as was lunch at McDonalds. So we had to go natural and fresh in our food choices and walk to the market to get them.

We are happy that we chose to continue this approach when we returned to the US, including the choice to breast feed. Breast feeding is the epitome of fresh and natural, and as much as possible, we chose food that was fresh and natural (fresh frozen is good and readily available in the US). We lived on one salary, and therefore could only afford McDonald's and other restaurants on vacation or other special occasions. We even decided to grind our own wheat and bake our own bread. It is not a requirement to do this in order to be healthy, but it was one more way for us to insure that our food was fresh and natural.

Good nutrition and good exercise during pregnancy, then, are the first and most practical ways we can support healthy brain development and therefore healthy kids. I should add because we live in America, and good diets are more difficult, it does make sense to take a quality multiple vitamin. Taking a daily multi-vitamin has been recommended in the *Journal of the American Medical Association*.[4] This provides some measure of dietary insurance, as it is very difficult to know everything that happens to our food in the process of getting it to our table.

One recommendation that I think is good, and that should be double checked with your physician, is that you vary your multi-vitamin. We do as a family. There is no certain agreement on the list of nutrients our bodies need, and it makes good sense to take different vitamins during the week with somewhat varied ingredients and varied levels of those ingredients.

In the Follower section, we will spend more time on exercise; however, there is at least one lesson we should apply from this section on nutrition to the coming section on Followers. A lot of schools will have you send a snack for your child. From what I see, most parents send factory products, not natural food. If you want the best for your child, make the effort to send fresh fruits and veggies. Most of the drinks I see in school, such as juice boxes and chocolate milk, have lots of sugar or artificial sweeteners. It's best to avoid too much of these for a growing body and brain.

Encyclopedia Britannica for the Womb?

I remember when I was told the baby can learn in the womb. He or she has a very active brain. He or she can hear, sense daylight and darkness, and make associations. Of course, this put visions in my head of racing out to the bookstore and buying the *Encyclopedia Britannica* and reading it by a crackling fire to my sweetie's swelling tummy. More than one of us has tried stuff like this with the very good intention of giving our kids a head start.

Whether it is playing music, reading, or reciting poetry, I'm reasonably sure that none of this is bad. It is helpful to understand, though, what the baby is likely learning while in mom's tummy. The baby will learn things more like how mom reacts to the world. Is it a safe or dangerous world? When someone comes over and visits, does mom stress out? We are finding that communication between mom and baby certainly takes place, but it is not to the extent that we can start teaching them the ABCs. The learning they experience is more on par with making associations.

When mom is stressed, her body will release stress hormones. These hormones will raise her blood pressure and heart rate. In extreme amounts, these hormones can interfere with digestion, growth, reproduction, and other aspects of health and learning.

Say Aunt Wilma pops over unannounced on a regular basis and generally introduces chaos into the family. Likely Wilma's boisterous, unexpected hello will release stress hormones in mom's body. If this is repeated enough, it is possible for the baby to learn from mom's reaction that Wilma is not considered a good thing. The baby brain can put together the sound of Wilma's voice and the rush of stress hormones.

Now, the baby is not actively thinking about this and making a conclusion; rather, this is an example of implicit learning—learning that takes place in the brain without being taught. If you were to add up everything that your baby will learn by age three or four, almost all of it would be the result of implicit learning, meaning they didn't intend to learn it. Literally, their brain makes them learn it without their permission or intention.

This is extremely important to keep in mind for parenting during this time. Your baby does not learn as a result of logical thinking or teaching. Your baby learns more by associations; what goes with what, who creates what reactions, and how mom feels in certain situations.

Let's imagine a household filled with chaos and fear. In this environment, those are what a baby will download. The fetus, and later the child, will tend to be filled with chaos and fear. We all know the cute little kindergartener who shows up at school the first day and creates chaos. *Let's poke Ryan. Let's get into anything that is not locked up. Let's ignore the teacher until she yells and frightens all the other kids*, etc. When sufficient chaos has been created, this kindergartener's little system now feels "normal." Why? Because that is what his or her life outside of school is like. They have gotten used to chaos being the normal state of being. Constructive order and play make them feel uncomfortable. It feels weird to them to follow instructions and behave.

Are they actually planning chaos? Not at all. The chaos is usually unintentional; it is the result of implicit learning. No one has sent them to a class called "Creating Chaos 101," although you'd swear they went and graduated as valedictorian. They have learned this way of responding because that is what they're around. We could use a metaphor to describe this kind of home. It is like building a nest in the middle of the freeway.

When was the last time you saw an animal build a nest at ground level in the middle of your local freeway? It doesn't happen, does it? Animals have a natural instinct to create a protective place for their offspring. The desire to nest normally takes an animal to an out-of-the-way, safe, quiet spot where they build a protected environment to raise their young. It takes place in a variety of ways, whether it's underground, high in the trees, with one parent devoted to the task or both working together. However it happens, a safe place is a priority, and a safe place is a foundational principle of FTF Parenting and healthy brain development.

Let's Make a Nest!

Usually the female has the strongest inner urge to create a safe place. This can appear to us guys as cuteness overload, but when our wives want to paint the baby's room, fill a crib with bunnies and pillows, and have us stay home on Friday night instead of going out with the guys, there is an enormously good reason–safety! It's all a part of creating a safe, brain-friendly, and developmentally appropriate place for our kids to grow.

What does this safe place look like?

We need to make our houses physically safe. It is time to baby-proof the house. X-acto knives need to be put away. Baby-proof door latches should be installed to keep Draino from being ingested, plastic plugs put in the electrical outlets, gates placed at the top of stairs (it's quite the adrenaline rush to learn this one the hard way, as we did), and dangerous or delicate things put out of the way of our little inquiring minds and hands. We need to assess Bowser and Garfield and make appropriate access and safety changes with our pets. Safety in the physical area our kids will live in is a top priority.

We also need to make our homes psychologically safe. There are decisions that we can make as parents to make our homes more brain-friendly places to live and grow up. Following are some excellent decisions and commitments we can make:

1) Make a commitment to be at home and involved in the parenting process.

A less stressed wife equals a less stressed and healthier kid. Your wife needs to know that her partner is committed to the parenting process and usually that means adjusting priorities. Being available to parent by being home is incredibly important for both the husband and wife, as well as the child.

I got my introduction to this when I was nineteen, and my dad kicked me out of the house (too much fighting with Mom). I went to live with my sister. She had two children under the age of three and was pregnant with a third. I was the youngest in my family, had only babysat once in my life (it was a disaster), and knew nothing about kids. Nor did I have any interest in kids, but I did admire and love my big sister.

I was genuinely blown away by how much work kids were. By the end of week one, I was already feeding kids and changing diapers. As the summer progressed, I found myself moving on to advanced skills, such as getting the oldest up in the middle of the night to go potty, thus contributing to a dry diaper through the night and successful toilet training. My sister's husband had to attend summer school in another part of the state and was gone Monday through Friday.

That summer made a huge impression on me. First, there was no doubt that kids were a lot of work, but second, the kids grew on me, and I came to love them and found that teamwork made a huge difference in handling the workload.

The best situation is for a husband and wife to be a team. Both should be committed to being available as much as possible to raise the kids together. This is not always possible. If not, grab a nephew, a mother-in-law, a grandfather, or whoever can be a part of your team. The job is 24-7, as the kids don't respect bank hours, and having a committed team will reduce workload and stress.

If you are the guy part of this team, as I was, you need to plan time at home. This may mean that you may temporarily have to give up some things, such as golf, like I did. Don't make your wife nag you and plead for you to be home. Be a man and figure out how you are going to support this new life. Put your wife at ease that you are committed by making your family a priority. Make yourself available, and spend time at home with the family. Men have an incredible ability to take care of things once they understand what needs to be done. Women need to take advantage of this skill by telling their guy what is needed. On the other hand, women tend to have a better innate knowledge of what young children need and shouldn't expect their guys to have this same understanding.

Ladies, you need to be explicit about what is needed. You should not hint, roll your eyes, or exhale loudly with a "how dumb can this guy be" look. You should admire and affirm your guy's commitment to be involved and help him understand what is needed with patience and love. We guys can be a tremendous part of your team, but most of us are slow on the uptake with babies. Not because we are stupid, but because much of this does not come as naturally to us as it does to females. While many girls were placing their dolls in baby carriages and playing house, we were conquering the fabled land of Zorn with ray blasters and blood-curdling screams.

In the case of kids, we men need to place our needs second and dedicate ourselves to our wives and our children. Men, this one decision will pay you huge dividends in the long run! The old adage has been proven more than once that if you set out to have a great life for yourself, you will miss it, but if you set out to make a great life for someone else, you will help them and find that you have made a great life for yourself as well.

Decision #1 for safe, less stressed kids: Commit to being available and involved from the beginning.

2) Commit to a schedule that is as consistent as possible.

For good brain development and growth, kids need sleep. This means a consistent bedtime each night. As we have said, learning in the Filler stage is not explicit. We can't sit our six month old down and say, "You need a good night's sleep and need to be in bed at

7 pm every night, so when you see the big hand blah, blah, blah...."
It just does not work that way. But if we put them to bed at 7 pm
every night, their internal body clock will adjust to that schedule.
If naps are at 10 am and 3 pm every day, their internal body clock
will adjust to that as well. If you eat dinner at 6 pm every night, not
only will their internal body clock adjust to that schedule, but their
digestive system will begin working about 15 to 20 minutes before
dinner, getting ready for what is coming, and they will digest their
food better and benefit nutritionally.

Too many of us these days want to drag our children into an
adult schedule so we can keep on doing whatever we want. This is
really tough on our children and will also be tough on us and our
families in the long run. I think most of us understand that if you
want to be a good baseball player, you need to practice baseball and
give up some competing interests. In the same way, if we want a
fulfilling and successful family, we have to give up at least some
competing adult interests. We and our children will benefit hugely
in the long run by a change as simple as staying home at night and
helping them get their sleep.

Having a schedule is also great preparation for school. As we will
see in the Follower section, schools generally thrive on schedules
and changing gears at expected times. By having a lifestyle with a
schedule, you begin to build this skill in your child. Alternatively,
if children have a chaotic schedule, their internal body clock will
be chaotic, their behavior will be more chaotic, and their life will
be more chaotic.

Decision #2 for safe, less stressed kids: Create as consistent a
schedule as possible.

3) Make the finances work.

This is not the time to be deep in debt and going crazy with two demanding full-time jobs. Do whatever needs to be done to reduce financial pressure. It seems like many Americans spend their lives trying to figure out how to get and finance more stuff. Hopefully, you've never had this habit. If you have, this is the best time to break it.

Our premarital counselor shared with us two financial principles that we decided to follow and that changed our lives in a beneficial way. First, as much as possible, he advised us, live on one salary. Do whatever it takes to support your lifestyle within that salary. Second, don't go into debt. Only buy what you can afford based on income, savings, and a sound financial plan.

By deciding to follow these two pieces of advice, all of a sudden we were largely out of the rat race. This doesn't mean we didn't want some of the rat race stuff, but we had another goal in mind, and that goal kept us from getting back into the rat race. We didn't drive new cars, we didn't go out to eat, we clipped coupons, we grew a garden, and we had a lot of fun together making all of this work. I took a break from playing golf, and our skis got hung up. We put together a bit of a savings account and often used weekly envelopes filled with cash to help us budget. We'd pay the monthly bills first, set a little bit aside for savings, then take everything left over and divide it into envelopes for the weeks in the month. We bought necessities first, and when the envelopes were empty, spending stopped for that week. It was that simple.

Occasionally, we forgot a bill that was coming up (like house taxes one year...ouch!), and that's when our savings account came in handy. When that happened, we'd dip into savings and then adjust our budget and began saving an extra amount each month to pay those taxes the next year. A modest savings account covers errors and helps make things work. We did not view our savings account as a way to get the stuff we always wanted; rather, it was a tool to help us make our new lifestyle with kids work.

Now I understand that this presents a problem for some of us, thinking, how can we give up these things for kids? We sat down and figured that even if we gave up certain "stuff" for ten years straight, we'd have another forty years, minimum, to do most, if not all, of it. And by giving it up, we gained huge benefits in raising our kids.

This brought the level of stress way down in our house. Our kids learned implicitly that the world was a fairly safe, enjoyable place where we didn't have to chase material stuff and had time for relationships. Remember that they learned this implicitly—not because we said it, but because we lived it.

Decision #3 for safe, less stressed kids: Commit to living within your means. Give up the rat race and enjoy.

4) Make your marriage relationship a priority.

If ever you need to be a team with your spouse, it is now. Usually, petty things divide us. Like who gets to decide what we spend our excess few dollars on, or who tells the "right" version of the day's exciting story to friends, or who is most tired, or whose in-laws get to stay in the guest bedroom.

If you haven't already learned how, it is time to make your team work and work well. Kids have an amazing ability to divide and conquer you later in life if you don't get this figured out. Let's be real. Just because you fell in love and have the most wonderful relationship that has ever existed in the world, that doesn't mean you lost your selfishness, your desire to be first, your desire to make your own decisions, or your tendency to think your perspective is the most important. If you don't work on correcting these tendencies, which will cause conflict between you and your sweetie, stress in your household will go up, and later in life your kids will likely use your selfish habits to play you against one another.

Another unfortunate result of conflict in our homes is that kids realize something is wrong and sometimes conclude they are the issue. In the Filler stage (and into the early Follower stage) their brains aren't developed enough to reflect on and think critically about what is happening. An unfortunate but possible message they will get when something is wrong in the family is that something is wrong with *me*. I (the child) am the cause of the problem. That is a sad situation. In terms of brain development, it is standard for a young child not to be able to distinguish himself from his surroundings (this is a skill we learn implicitly). It is common for a child to feel sick when mommy feels sick. So if our house is in conflict, it is very possible for a child to have the sense planted deep within them that he or she is the problem, the source of the conflict.

Because of this, more than you need a new computer in the house, or the right version of the story told to friends, or a declaration of who wins the "most tired" award, or the "right guest" in the guest bedroom, your children need parents who learn to work together, who learn to give up selfish desires, who realize there is so much more to life than "me," and who fill the house with love. Especially love for each other.

At the Filler stage in life, if we surround our kids with a cooperative, loving relationship in which people are valued, given attention, and kept safe; they will download cooperation, love, and a feeling of being safe and valued into their brains. This is not all we need to do, but it is the majority of what we need to do.

Decision #4 for safe, less stressed kids: Love and support your spouse or significant other in an unselfish way.

5) Turn off the TV.

Sorry to pick specifically on TV, but it is a psychological toxin for young minds. In fact, I love TV because it is such a good example of what not to do with a young mind. First, TV is a dangerous place. People are always getting killed, accidents are happening, scary people are chasing other people, age inappropriate behavior is all over the place, lists of worrisome side effects are being read, and humor is largely composed of people putting other people down. You and I have the ability to think critically about TV. If we see something inappropriate we can think, *That was entirely unfair and not right for her to treat him like that.* A little child does not have this ability. They download in the Filler stage.

Second, it is bad for brain development. According to researchers, your child's chances of being diagnosed with ADHD (Attention Deficit Hyperactivity Disorder) goes up 10 percent with every hour of TV you let them watch a day when they are very young.[5] TV also supplies everything (visual, auditory, imagination) so the brain gets very little exercise. TV does not encourage us to use our imaginations, our muscles, or anything really. The only skill that really gets built is the ability to sit and stare.

Being motionless is really bad for brain development and learning. The part of your brain that gives you a coordinated body, your cerebellum, also appears to coordinate your thoughts. Literally. Even though the cerebellum is only 10 percent of the brain's weight, it has about 40 percent of the brain's neurons. It sits in the back of our head and develops early through activity.

Have you noted how all young mammals like to roughhouse and play? Kittens, puppies, cubs, and kids love to do this. This play not only teaches physical skills but also develops the cerebellum. It appears that the better the cerebellum is developed, the better the areas of the brain will be coordinated as they come online throughout our kids' lives, and the better they will be able to think. Kids need dedicated time for running and jumping, hanging upside down, and throwing water balloons at each other. Activity also reduces toxic brain chemicals and produces beneficial brain chemicals that are protective and encourage growth.

TV and most video games suck the desire to be active and play right out of our kids. They can sit for hours on end doing nothing. Our little kids really, really, really don't need TV.

To be honest, however, sometimes mom and/or dad are the ones who need TV. By this, I mean that mom and dad need the break that TV can bring. When it has been a tough day, everything has gone wrong, and your mental state is not good, it is helpful from time to time to plug in a decent DVD and hypnotize the kids for thirty minutes while you regain your composure, finish a project, or relax. Keep this as an option for you while keeping TV to a minimum with young brains.

My wife and I let our kids watch a little TV. Typically, as I explained above, it was to give us a break and involved a familiar video. We didn't even allow *Sesame Street*, which was a popular show when our kids were young. My wife is an educator, and even before there were studies showing that TV was too fast-paced for good brain development, she decided that the pace of *Sesame Street* was not conducive to the skill of being able to pay attention. So there was no *Sesame Street* in our house.

Our most entertaining story of the effect of TV came from the incident that we refer to as "Dr. Dobson teaching our children to steal." If you are not familiar with Dr. Dobson, he promotes conservative values from a religious perspective. Dr. Dobson did not personally teach our kids to steal, but we bought a video that came from his organization. In that video, two people were stealing things and, of course, the moral of the story (if you followed the story all the way through) was that stealing was bad. What did our kids learn?

My wife took the kids for a walk after watching that video for the first time, and she was amazed to hear the kids saying, "Let's steal this" or "Let's steal that." She put two and two together and realized the video had had an effect. It had never crossed our kids' minds to steal anything until the video from Dr. Dobson's organization introduced the idea. Now we had two kids ready to rip things off.

Because my wife was a stay at home mom (we believe it is always the best choice to have a parent able to devote themselves to the child's development in the early, formative years, if you can manage it financially), she was intimately involved with all the things the kids were learning. She could address this "misunderstanding" in the moment and reinforce the lesson that the video intended. In hindsight, was it the best choice to allow the kids to watch this video? Let me answer this way.

Kids will eventually learn about stealing. It is best to learn about something like stealing in the Follower stage rather than the Filler/early Follower stage. The further a child is into the Follower stage, the more critically they can think about what they are learning, and the more able they are to understand and listen to your perspective on that issue. What is learned in the Filler stage and early Follower stage seems to become more an unconscious part of their lives because they simply download these ideas and attitudes. TV is not good from this perspective.

Our kids will eventually need to be exposed to and understand all aspects of life, the good and the bad. The key for good brain development is tackling these things at the right time, when brains are capable of dealing with the situation. The problem with TV is that it exposes kids' brains to all of it, all at once, without any thought of age appropriateness. For the sake of your kids during the Filler and early Follower stage, make decision #5.

Decision #5: Turn off the TV.

I hope that you are catching the main idea here. The atmosphere you set in your home (your nest) is critical. As a husband and wife team, you are to protect that environment and make it a physically and psychologically safe place for your child. That is the priority. You need to take some time to think about your life situation and identify what things create excess stress.

As noted earlier, if Aunt Wilma shows up unexpectedly and creates chaos, or if a mother-in-law has a habit of intimidating her daughter-in-law, you need to control those situations. One good way is to be up front about the problem and limit contact if necessary.

You can be indirect with someone who may unknowingly create chaos and say something like the following. "As you know, we now have little Buster in the house, and we need you to call and see if it is a good time to stop by. If it is not, we will tell you." This will allow you to limit the contact. Make sure you lock the front door, and the first time he or she drops by unannounced, don't let the offender in. He or she will learn.

You can be direct and work to inform the offenders. "Mom, you put Teresa ill at ease when you criticize how she keeps house. I can't have that, so drop the criticism." Then you need to be present when Mom is around. If Mom is being critical, point out, "Mom, that is being critical." And if Mom can't give it up, limit the contact.

Just as any bird has the innate sense to build a safe nest as far away from danger as possible, we should have that same sense. The Filler stage is not a time to "expose" our kids to reality. That exposure should take place gradually in the next stage (the Follower stage) when you can talk with them and think with them about the meaning of events and the appropriate responses to what we find in our world.

Helping Fill the Filler Stage

So far, we talked about building a protective atmosphere as the main thing we can do in the Filler stage. While this is true, there is more we can do. We will use some specific topics to illustrate this.

Studies in the development of language capabilities can give us some insight into what is going on in our kids' heads. Dr. Patricia Kuhl at the University of Washington has done some amazing work in how our children learn languages and what the important factors are.[6]

As I pointed out earlier in this book, between the ages of six and twelve months, a part of the brain comes online that categorizes and memorizes the sounds the baby is hearing and creates a library. If your baby is hearing English, all the basic sounds of the English language will be stored so that the baby can use this capability both to understand and speak English. If your baby hears Chinese, the basic sounds of Chinese will be stored.

One of the most fascinating parts of this experiment was work to show whether or not you can lay the foundation for learning a foreign language by playing a foreign language tape or DVD to an infant. One of the early findings of this research determined an amount of time that would cause the sounds of a language to be stored in a child's brain. The study determined that if you had a live native speaker read stories in their language for a relatively brief period each week during the six to twelve month period, those sounds would be recognized and stored by the brain.

The researchers then pursued the question, "Can we just play a tape?" Groups were set up that had a live native speaker, a very well done DVD of the same native speaker, and an audio tape. The results were very informative. The live native speaker caused the children's brains to learn the sounds, the audio tape did not.

The amazing thing was that the well-produced DVD did not create learning either. The infant needed a real person to implicitly learn the sounds of a language.

This pattern has not been tested as clearly in other areas, but I will conclude that for the best learning, an infant needs you and other "real" people. In all areas of learning at this age and stage of life, the best teacher is you, your spouse, and your extended family and friends. This can be supplemented with recorded songs and material, but the main learning comes with real people spending time with your child. The most important teacher is you.

What does brain friendly teaching mean in the Filler stage? It first means spending time with your child. It means understanding that you are the most important source of learning for your child. It means understanding that more than our child needs to know a bunch of facts, they need to make the right associations. We teach them these associations by what we do.

- What happens just because you're our baby? You are loved and accepted.
- What happens when the baby has a need (hungry, dirty diaper, tired)? We meet that need.
- What happens when the baby accomplishes something (first step, etc.)? We get all excited.
- What happens when the baby does something good? We respond with praise for a good choice.
- What happens when our child wants to play? We engage in play or put them in a good situation to play.
- What happens when the baby does something inappropriate? We show the impact and/or correct the behavior.

- What happens when our child pushes safe limits? We set and enforce safe limits.

- What happens when mom or dad get upset or fight? We cool down, apologize, and make up.

- What happens when someone makes a mistake? We don't blame but try and learn something and give it another go.

Learning at this stage is almost all about what we do and say, the example we set. It is not whether we buy the right books, have the DVDs that will give them a head start, or send them to the right class. What we do, say, and experience together is more than sufficient to fill up what they need to learn. So consider yourself and your partner the most technologically advanced learning device your Filler will ever need.

Some incredibly interesting studies have taken place in rodents and primates that underline how important parents are to their infants. A series of studies in rats found that rats that were handled by humans for a few minutes a day learned better, handled stress better, and were healthier than rats not handled by humans.[7]

The scientists then went the next step. If a little bit of handling is good, then a lot of handling should be better. They then had a group of rat infants handled for 180 minutes (3 hours) a day. They found that these rats learned worse, handled stress worse, and were less healthy than rats not handled by humans. Obviously this result created a question: What was really going on? Do rats have a built-in human time limit? Only so much human exposure is good for them?

Not at all. The scientists were looking at the wrong interaction. What was really happening was that if a baby rat (pup) was taken away from his mom for a few minutes, the mom was more attentive to the pup when it was returned. In fact the short separation induced mild stress that was resolved through more licking and more attention by mom. If the pup was taken away for too long, while mom still paid attention to the pup, the environmental separation was too long and created too much stress. It appears then that some stress resolved by attentive parental care is good. Stress will normally happen in the parenting of our kids, because things will go wrong. The key is that we are there to help resolve the problems and comfort our kids.

So it wasn't the human handling that primarily affected the rats; it was mom's attentive care that ameliorated environmental stress. Further research has indicated similar results in primates.[8] The attentive care of parents in resolving mild stress (especially by the mother) makes healthier, less stressed offspring that are better able to learn. This finding is huge, especially when you consider what science taught us at the beginning of the 20th century.

My dad grew up early in the 20th century and told me about a pop psychologist who had a tremendous influence on parenting. His name was Luther Holt, and my dad said he taught parents things like you shouldn't hug your children but should instead greet them formally with a handshake, and that you could ruin a baby by picking it up when it cried. This sort of formal distance dominated a lot of families, and research is now showing that this approach can actually have a negative effect on our ability to learn, handle stress, and be healthy even into our adult years.

This research underlines that our Fillers need us and our care. Don't worry about spoiling an infant and don't worry that things will go wrong. Rather focus on providing attentive care. What Fillers need more than anything is for parents to arrange their lives so that they can give them that good attentive care and love them deeply. To do this well, we may need to deal with fears in the Filler stage. Too much fear, as I said earlier, drives love from our homes.

Chapter 4

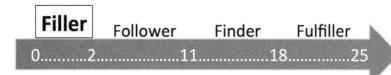

Filler	Follower	Finder	Fulfiller
0..........2....................11....................18..............25			

Fear and the Filler Stage

T he first child always takes parents into unchartered territory. While many others have gone through the experience of child rearing, we haven't. It is absolutely normal to have fears, and it is best to admit those fears up front and discuss them. Fear that is not handled correctly will create stress in the home and will bring the negative consequences of stress.

This, of course, implies that you recognize your fears or stress. If you are like me, I didn't have a clue that I was stressed to the max until I had to get a physical for soccer and visited my college clinic as a sophomore. A friendly nurse took my blood pressure and made one of those odd noises that I don't think medical people are supposed to make. After taking my blood pressure a second time, she announced it was 185 over 140.

She had me commit to coming back on a regular basis. Over the next six months of visits I began to learn that I was highly stressed with a lot of internal fears and confusion. I had gotten to the point where I didn't know what it felt like to be relaxed and calm on the inside. As I learned to relax over those months, my blood pressure slowly returned to a healthy 120/80. Although it would take years to deal with some of my particular fears and stressors, I began to develop an internal sense of when things were wrong. Having this sense and trusting it, was incredibly helpful in identifying my fears and sources of stress.

Whether or not you have a good internal sense of when you are stressed or fearful, it is a valuable exercise to consider what you might fear or what might stress you in the child raising process. It is far better to recognize fear and stress and work with them, than to have them unrecognized and to not understand their negative effects.

First of all, remember that fear in small amounts is a good thing; we call it caution. Every one of us has areas in our brain that caution us against doing stupid things. People in whom these areas of the brain don't work well often die early. We've all been passed by the guy doing 90 or 100 miles per hour down the freeway. Areas of the brain like the amygdala and basal ganglia likely aren't working well in that driver's head. So if our brains are working correctly, we should feel caution and fear in appropriate circumstances.

The unknown will always cause a sense of caution. Ever since you were young, stepping into a dark alley, or getting ready for your first recital, caused your brain to put your body on alert! A lot of us shouldn't expect anything different with having a first baby. It could be that having a baby has been something you've wanted forever, and you've had plenty of experience around kids. In this case, there may be no caution or fear. But even then you should understand that for most of us, the first time we do something causes caution or fear. So don't think it's weird that your partner would have fears about having and raising kids.

The best thing to do is admit any fears openly to yourself and to your spouse. Then do what we should do with fears. Let them help us understand the danger and then use our heads to make the right decision.

It's like you're at Disneyland, looking up at Screaming California (their big roller coaster), feeling that you could never survive the ride. Then you see someone at least ten years younger than you get off the ride with a huge smile on his face, talking about how great it was. That starts you thinking. He did it. He's not dead. In fact he looks happy. With a certain amount of butterflies in your stomach, you decide to go. As you wait in line, you feel like running away, but you hang tough.

Finally, you're there at the head of the line. A friendly Disneyland employee helps you by pulling down the safety bar and checking it, and then you're on your way. As you look at the first hill drawing near, you're tempted to close your eyes, but you keep them open. The first hill is a doozy, and your stomach is left at the top, but it's not as bad as you thought. In fact, by the time you round the last corner and come to a screeching halt, you've decided it's fun.

This is life. Crying in kindergarten because your loving, familiar mom left you in your teacher's care. Feeling totally out of place in middle school and hating to walk down the hall. Stepping out onto the football practice field in high school and realizing everyone is a lot bigger than you thought and feeling a certain amount of anticipation mixed with apprehension as you begin your first contact drills. Standing awkwardly on the front porch of your date's house wondering how you should say goodbye. Realizing that you've chosen a much tougher rock climb than you thought, but you're committed, and you've got to go on.

This is life. Facing something new, different, uncomfortable, or challenging and taking it on; finding benefits as you work through it. Fear can get in the way. We all know someone who is stuck in a certain part of their life. School was a bad experience so they dropped out and never graduated. A girl turned them down, so they never asked anyone else out for a date. They failed at a sport, so they never turned out for any other sport. They were embarrassed in front of a class, so they never take an opportunity to perform, even though they secretly wish to.

This is the good and the bad side of fear. Fear and caution should make us think, but they should never control our actions. Let's say you had a bad experience in front of class, so every time an opportunity came up to try out for a play you didn't do it, even though you want to. You should think it through. You should even write down your fears and then have a discussion with them.

Let's say you wrote, "I didn't audition for the play because I will forget my lines in front of everyone and fail." This was my first experience in a play. The curtain opened, and I had the first line. Could I remember it? No! I sat there stone quiet. But you know what? The person closest to me whispered the first few words, and I was off. It happens, but since when should the possibility of failure stop us? It shouldn't.

Talk back to your fear. Argue with it. "Yes, I may forget a line, but if I do, someone will help me out." "I may be embarrassed, but I won't be alone because other people have forgotten lines." "I might learn what to do when I forget a line and be a better actor in the long run." When you talk back to your fears, your decision should be based on your thinking and your sense of caution, not just your sense of caution. Fear and caution are your brain's way of saying, "First, make sure you're safe, and then think about what to do."

This is true in parenting. Write down your fear. "Having a child means I won't be able to get together with my buddies, and I will lose their friendship." "Having a child means I won't be able to devote as much time to my job, and I won't advance like I want." "What if I mess up my child like my parents did?" Then talk back to the fear.

If you're a guy, your conversation may go this way, "It is true I may have less time with my buddies,

- but I will have more time with my wife and child."
- but I will still have opportunities to spend time with buddies."
- but some of them are getting married and having kids, so we will have that in common and this might strengthen our friendship."
- but we can still plan a weekend get-away from time to time."

You may have concerns about your career, "True, if I have children and stay home to raise them, I may not advance as quickly in my job,

- but after the children are in school, I will have some free time to devote to my career."

- but even if I don't work until the last one is 16, I will still have more than twenty years to pursue my career."
- but I'm told that people don't regret missing a job advancement in the end, but they do regret not building a strong relationship with their kids."

You may have concerns about your ability to parent, "True, I could make mistakes that negatively affect my child like my parents did,

- but I've learned some things to avoid and can probably do a better job."
- but I can be open and talk about it like I wish my parents would have and that will be a great help."
- but there are a lot of materials (like this book) and people to help, and if I take advantage of them that will make a difference for the better."

In other words, we embrace the fear not to stop us, as fears often do, but to make us think through the situation. Usually when we do that, we come up with some good solutions. Be thankful for fear! Allow fear to motivate some good thinking and good discussion. Then act on what you decide.

It may be you fear starting a family because you aren't financially prepared and wonder whether you should change jobs. Fear leading to good thinking may cause you to postpone having a child for a couple of years while you get your finances together or find a more suitable job. This would be a good result of the kind of thinking and positive action that can come from facing our fears.

If we admit our fears and think about them, we usually benefit ourselves and those around us. The danger is not that we have fears and that things may go wrong; the real danger is that we won't think through our fears and make thoughtful decisions about what to do. When that happens, we end up with feelings like regret and resentment. We resent having to be home on Friday night because we've never thought of the benefits of having a family; we've only feared what we might lose. We resent not advancing in our career because we've never thought through this fear. When these fears control you, it is difficult to really say to your baby, "You are loved and accepted no matter what," and attitudes based on fear can accentuate fears in your child.

Not dealing with fear then leaves it as a powerful part of yourself and family. This attitude of fear can be picked up by our child though it is often expressed in different ways. It could be expressed as fear of the dark, fear of mom or dad leaving, or fear of doing new things. Because kids learn implicitly in the Filler stage, our fearful attitude can become a fearful attitude in them. Better to face our fears, think through them, and choose to have kids knowing that there will be difficulties, but that the journey, like any other, will be well worth it.

For a lot of us, if we begin this process of examining our fears, it will become apparent that fear has been making too many decisions for us. Begin to make better decisions by facing your fears and talking back to them. For some of us those fears may be paralyzing, and we can't talk our way out of them for whatever reason. If so, get help from a counselor. During my more than fifty years, I have sought help from a counselor a number of times, and in each case that help has been very valuable.

Filler – Summing It Up:

What have we said very briefly about the Filler stage?

- It is from conception until about two years old. Each child differs somewhat.

- It is characterized by the child learning through downloading information and skills from what is going on around them (implicit learning).

- Our job is to work with others to build a safe place for our child and our family. It needs to be both physically and emotionally safe.

  o This involves making places safe from objects or situations that can hurt the child.

  o This involves learning about and providing excellent nutrition for the child (they don't need soda).

  o This involves limiting what the child is exposed to (turn off the TV...have I said that before?).

  o This involves the people around the child behaving in loving and responsible ways. If they won't, we limit or prohibit contact or get help.

- We can actively contribute to what fills our children's brains. Our reactions and behavior will show them ways to respond and how to feel about life. If we work on positive and constructive reactions and behaviors, this will build those same reactions and behaviors in our children.

- We need to face our fears. Uncontrolled or long-term fears and anxiety affect our behavior and will physically affect our child directly through stress hormones during pregnancy and indirectly during the Filler years. If fear motivates us, fear will likely become a part of our child's life. I think it is important to point out that some children's temperaments are more fearful than others. Children will naturally have some fears. The key question however is, "Have I dealt with my own fears?" If so, that learning and experience will be the basis of helping your children deal with their fears.

From a healthy brain standpoint, all of these principles will continue into the next stage, but the child will begin changing in significant ways, bringing about a new stage of parenting that I call the Follower stage.

Chapter 5

Follower Part I

This stage begins an amazing time of life. I love all of the stages, but if you enjoy being a parent and are devoted to the task of parenting, the Follower stage is built for you. The parts of your child's brain that make them want to learn and, even more, to actively learn from you are coming online. As I have already said, this stage begins about at the age of two or three and lasts until approximately age eleven (give or take a couple of years).

At this point, assuming all things are normal, your child is bonded to you, and it is natural for him or her to want to follow you, emulate you, and copy you. Many kids can remember wanting to marry their mom or dad. They want to spend time with you. Their brains are wired to be attached to you and to pattern their behavior and attitudes after yours. Systems such as mirror neurons and chemicals such as oxytocin support this wiring and their desire to follow you. This is the human version of all the little ducklings lining up behind momma duck and following. The main parental job in this stage is to be present and involved. Do things together!

Since your child is designed to allow you to be the biggest influence in their lives during the Follower years (as is also true in the Filler years), this stage naturally has a great chance of success. Your presence and involvement as a parent goes a long way toward successful parenting. There are two main ways for you to mess this up: 1) be a really bad example to follow, or 2) not be there. If you have horrible habits in your life, have given up changing for the better, and don't care if your kids inherit your same problems, it is really difficult to do a decent job of parenting. It is also difficult if you hand over your parenting time to the TV or are simply absent.

Only a few things are needed to succeed at this stage, 1) want to do a good job, 2) be present and involved, and 3) turn off the TV and video games to increase time together and to limit these harmful influences. Even I found that I could do these things. Wanting good things for my kids seemed natural, finding my way home every night after work was easy, and fortunately the on and off button on the TV remote control were the same button, so even that did not present a great challenge.

Did I always do a good job? No. But kids are actually pretty durable. You can't avoid making mistakes with your kids, but as I say throughout this book, mistakes are good. Mistakes are how we learn. It is rare to accomplish something new perfectly the first time. If we understand that the brain learns best through making errors and correcting them, we will embrace mistakes as the normal learning process and relax.

I embraced the fact that mistakes would happen, that we could all learn from mistakes together, and decided not to worry. I committed to being with the family in the evenings and on the weekends. I showed love and support for the kids' mom and with a willingness to play horsey or whatever the kids wanted, I had all the basics I needed for good parenting at this stage. Add to this a teachable attitude, and I was on my way to becoming even better!

Beyond being present and involved, can we add some skills to this that will help? Certainly, we can do things that will even make us more effective in parenting our kids in brain-compatible ways! I'd like to suggest we begin with four areas: 1) learning how we can help wire our kids' brains, 2) learning to use State Management, 3) understanding school readiness, and 4) describing our child's world as we live life together.

Wiring our Kids' Brains

To understand how our kids' brains get wired, we are going to use a simple connection idea, add to that a short discussion of what happens when an area of the brain comes online, and then use some illustrations to see how this all works.

Let's begin with the connection idea. To help our understanding of what is going on in our kid's head at about three years of age in a very simple way, we are going to use the illustration of four sets of plugs. The different sets of plugs represent:

1. The parts of the brain that make the body move (Movement).
2. The parts of the brain that decide (Decisions).

3. The parts of the brain that reward us (Reward).
4. The parts of the brain that feel (Feelings).

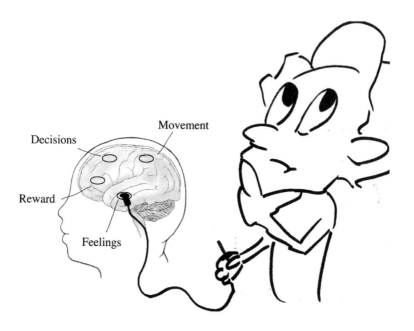

So we've got movement, decisions, reward, and feelings. All of these have their primary control in different areas of the brain. Now imagine a series of wires that connect them in a variety of combinations.

It is incredibly important to understand that while our genes supply a gazoodle of potential brain connections, they do not hook them all up. Certain things like breathing or jumping when startled get hooked up automatically (good news!), but most connections are not automatic. In fact, the majority of the connections in our brains are "hooked up" by what we are exposed to, what happens to us, what we focus on, and what choices we make. While the brain automatically supplies potential connections, our experience hooks most of them up. How we relate to our kids, and the experiences and influences we allow them to be exposed to, are incredibly powerful in affecting their brain development.

Another idea to expand on is one we referred to earlier: parts of the brain come online over time. One misunderstanding that can come from the word online is that parts of the brain don't work before they come online. This is not true. Using any part of the brain will establish connections, and that part of the brain can become more effective. So even if an area of the brain is not online, using that area will strengthen it and help it work better. For example, the primary decision-making part of the brain (frontal cortex) is not online in the Follower stage; however, if we have our children use it through choices, decision making, and goal-setting, it will improve with use. Later in life when this area of the brain *does* come fully online, it will work faster, and it will benefit greatly from the connections that have already been established.

Along with areas coming online, the brain enters a relatively stable period of growth until around age eleven. This means that your child will have a fairly predictable pattern of learning what you teach them and of following the examples of people they're around. After time, with the right influences, this will make them seem like sensible little adults. They aren't adults, and we all know that, but with good examples to follow, good teaching, and encouragement, their brains are very capable of following and behaving like an adult in many ways. This ability is an advantage, especially as we discuss choices and goal setting at the end of this section, but it can also be a disadvantage to us in our parenting if we don't understand why we see the appearance of adult behavior in a child.

It is common for conscientious parents to believe that they've got this wonderful, sensible, child well on his way to adulthood in fifth grade, only to feel by seventh grade that the child has regressed and decided to rebel against them and all they have taught. This stark change, which we will deal with in the Finder stage, makes no sense until you realize how the brain develops. In the Follower stage, children are not little adults, no matter how well they behave; rather, they are children very adept at learning from and following your example. We, as parents, are very influential in how their brains get wired, and a basic understanding of this process will be incredibly helpful.

Let's take all of this (plugs, wiring, areas coming online, and relative stability) and see how it works in some examples. The plugs that control the body's movement start to come online relatively early, and a jumble of wires exist in the brain, waiting to get hooked up. Part of the natural playfulness in children, puppies, or any other animal motivates their bodies to move so that the wiring can make the right connections. This connecting happens in a number of ways. One is to literally make a new wire (a new brain cell) that is used to make connections. One is to make new connections with existing wires (brain cells have thousands of connection possibilities). One way is to strengthen already existing connections (this makes the connections work better).

At the same time, parts of the brain are coming online. So when a baby is motivated to move, that makes connections. When they learn to walk all of a sudden, this is a good indicator that the area of their brain controlling walking just came online and became more efficient. If you restrained a baby and didn't allow him to move and try to walk, he wouldn't learn to walk because the connections wouldn't be made.

Infants have a natural aptitude to learn to walk, but opportunities to try, fail, and try again will wire the brain so that they can walk. Each time they fall, they get back up again. You've seen the trial and error approach as they take a few steps and fall, until finally they can run into a waiting parent's arms. To summarize this using our illustration, our brain is naturally supplied with wires and plugs, and we hook most of them up through experience.

Now imagine your child is two or three years old. He loves to move and that indicates that the movement parts of his brain are online. So his movement plug is having wires connected to it. His feelings plug is also somewhat connected. If he gets tired, he feels cranky, and his behavior through whining tells you he needs a nap. His reward plug is also somewhat connected and he responds to praise, to attention, to pleasing mom or dad, and feels good about doing those things. What is not well-connected is his decision maker. At this stage he just follows whatever attracts him and blurts out whatever he feels. Your guidance as parents and what you allow him to do will affect how these parts of his brain get wired.

Here is a great example. Buster is at the checkout counter and sees candy. He expresses an immediate feeling, "I want some candy." Mom responds, "It's too close to lunch. You can't have any candy." Buster's feelings overwhelm him, and he throws himself on the floor, kicking and screaming, "But I want candy."

This is a really critical point. Buster is just acting as he is wired. Buster is not maliciously planning to take over control of the family. Buster has not been staying up all night thinking, *If I socially embarrass my parents in the right situations, I can get whatever I want.* Buster did not decide to throw himself on the floor and wail in order to exercise dominance. Buster is simply showing that his emotional wiring is well connected to his movement wiring. He doesn't feel good about what just happened, and this is a predictable way for his body to show those feelings. This is actually a good thing.

You want these systems well connected early in life. If his emotional system says, "Be afraid. There is a large dog threatening you," his body needs to react immediately. You do not want him going into a deep mental deliberation about this. Hopefully he will cry out, and you will hear and respond and come and save him. This is a great thing, and his basic emotions and body ought to be closely connected to help keep him safe.

But getting candy is not a safety issue. In fact, what happens in the next few moments will begin to train Buster's brain. If Buster's behavior is rewarded through the wrong response, his parents can actually train Buster to premeditate falling on the floor and screaming to influence them (this is a bad thing) or, by making the right response, they can head him toward becoming a good decision maker who doesn't use temper tantrums to get his way.

If Buster's parents are smart, they will realize the checkout counter episode (or any similar episode) is a great opportunity to make the rest of their lives easier. Instead of freaking out when Buster explodes, they can respond internally, "This is my chance to wire his brain and have an easier job in the future. I like less work!" I think most of us like less work. The right decision in this situation may be a bit more work now, but it will mean much less work in the future. Let's look at some scenarios and see what might happen.

Scenario #1: Buster asks for candy, Mom says no, Buster screams, Mom complies, Buster eats the tasty candy. Let's think about what connections are being made. Buster had a feeling, and though the parent knows it is not best for the child, she reacts to the way Buster's body is already wired and complies. At this point, she has just strengthened that connection. When Buster eats the candy, he feels rewarded, further strengthening the connection.

What has she done? She has just strengthened the connection between the movement plug, the feelings plug, and the rewards plug for Buster to get his way by a throwing a tantrum and feel good about it. She has just taught him that if he is disappointed, he should respond with the first desire he feels (tantrum) and he will get rewarded and feel good.

At this point, any of us who have done this should walk over to the mirror and ask ourselves, "Is this what we want?" Think about it: We are possibly creating a social deviant at the checkout counter at our local grocery store using candy. All because of how we respond to our children. Wow! By not understanding what is going on, we make a wrong decision. The kid asks, and we know it's not the best, but then he screams, and we realize that four people behind us are watching. We feel embarrassed and know if we just give the kid candy, he'll shut up. We don't want a scene, so we do the wrong thing and wire their brain in the wrong way.

This doesn't seem to be a problem in a three year old. The episode is over quickly, and the kid is cute and small and happy. But if we consistently train this way, this scenario gets really scary in middle school. The kid is almost as big as we are and still throws a fit to get his way. Now all of a sudden, this is not cute; it is threatening, and the path to correct it is long and difficult. We have unwittingly wired his brain since age three to behave this way. It is difficult (but possible) to undo this wiring. However, it is by far best and easiest to encourage the right wiring in the first place.

What is missing in this scenario is the ability of the child to control himself. We as parents provide that capability and teach our children to control themselves over time. Kids don't come equipped with self-control and good decision making. Let's follow the same scenario but handle it differently.

Scenario #2: Buster asks, and Mom affirms what he's feeling. "You'd like a candy bar, wouldn't you?" Buster looks at her with big eyes that plead yes. "You have a choice, Buster. It's lunchtime, so you can pick a candy bar, and we will share it after lunch, or we can leave the candy bar on the shelf."

Now, Buster has been given the opportunity to exercise the decision part of his brain. If it goes well, Buster will say, "Let's pick a candy bar." Mom reminds him, "You can't have it until after lunch." Buster picks the candy bar (making a choice is an excellent brain exercise) and then watches Mom pack it in the bag and delays his want to eat it for now (delaying gratification is also an excellent brain exercise). He then eats the candy bar and is rewarded after lunch for making the decision to listen to Mom and wait.

This scenario worked on wiring his brain differently. The emotional and reward areas of the brain have been more strongly connected to the decision part. This is really good. This leads to a middle school student who actually thinks before he or she explodes. This is a capability we will come to appreciate in our middle school kids to the extent it is developed. (Trust me; they will still explode at times. We will learn why later.)

We as parents direct the wiring of our kids' brains. If they are going to become good at making decisions, it will be because we give them decisions to make and help them make those decisions. If they are going to become good at doing the right thing, it will be because we reward them for doing the right thing. How else might this situation take place?

Scenario #3: Buster asks, and in a tired voice Mom says, "No! no candy." Buster screams and falls to the floor. This is the critical point. Mom's handling of this will determine if Buster is trained whether screaming is the right way to go or not.

Here's how we handled it as parents. Buster's reaction would remind us that we are parents, and we need to parent. We would bend down and give Buster a choice. "Buster, you can stop screaming, and we can talk about the candy bar, or you can keep screaming, not get a candy bar, and I will discipline you." If Buster kept screaming and didn't respond, in sympathy to all behind us in line and in keeping with good parenting, we would pick up little Buster, give him a nice caring parental hug, say to him in a firm voice, "Screaming does not get you what you want," and pinch his little thigh.

To all observing, we have just intervened, picked up and hugged our poor little out-of-control child, and the child just started crying harder. They had no idea we pinched him.

What did we just wire? "Buster, when you react without thinking, that choice will likely have an unpleasant consequence." As we know, reacting without thinking generally provides unpleasant consequences throughout our whole life. When parents intervene as we did, we force a developing brain to learn skills for making good choices in the long run. The next time Buster is motivated to fall down and scream in a store over a candy bar, implicit learning will remind him that it did not go well last time, and he needs to think about his response. Tantrums may occur a number of times, but Buster will eventually get the message.

Buster will realize that a temper tantrum is a choice that brings consequences. If the consequences aren't what he wants, he will learn to change his choices. This response on our part wires the decision-making part of his brain to be more active in directing his movement part. The direct connection between strong feelings and throwing a temper tantrum will now have some strengthened connections to the deciding part of the brain, meaning that Buster may hesitate and choose a different option the next time he feels like throwing himself on the floor and screaming.

Discomfort as a Teaching Tool

Now I understand that I have suggested using discomfort (a pinch) as a teaching tool. This may result in riots in New Delhi, sit-ins at the White House, and protests in the streets of London.

To many, this is not politically correct. I assure you that pain, used correctly, is absolutely fine. Discomfort is misunderstood by so many. It is one of nature's most basic ways of teaching a lesson.

If you spend too much time in the sun, you will feel the sunburn. If you fail to attend to a recurring stomach ache, you may end up with an ulcer. I drank the hot paraffin off the top of a canning jar as a child and learned through pain to never do that again. Pain is admittedly not pleasant, but it is a fundamental tool that nature uses to teach lessons. In fact it is the universally understood, most basic signal of danger to the brain. It is a mistake for our society to attempt to remove this teaching tool from a parent's toolbox.

I learned the active use of pain partially from my Norwegian Elkhound, Thora. Our family raised puppies, and I was the main caretaker. I saw Thora more than once give a little nip when a puppy wanted to run someplace dangerous or the puppy bit too hard when nursing. I have even seen a mother deer pick up her hoof and plant it squarely on her fawn's haunches for doing something the doe considered dangerous.

There is a time when children can't reason and can't respond appropriately to reason. We are being kind when we appropriately use discomfort or pain to keep them safe, and this helps them by adding meaning to our words. To expect very young children to understand reason and apply it in the future when they are not capable from a brain development standpoint is unkind and can be dangerous.

Where we get confused in this area is when we mix anger and discipline that uses pain. We should never discipline a child out of anger. If we are angry, we need to solve our anger problem first and then consider the appropriate teaching tool. The pinch we gave Buster was not hard enough to cause a bruise, and was probably not even hard enough for the pain to last longer than a few seconds.

What I hope you see is that a little bit of thoughtful discipline that involves some discomfort at this stage can save Buster a huge amount of pain in the future. I want to emphasize that one mistake we make as parents is to think that "I will simply reason with the child and they will cooperate." If you understand brain development, this is unreasonable on our part. Good reasoning is something that takes years to build into your child's life as they grow. It does not exist at age two or three. Once a child is old enough to reason, the punishment should also evolve to an age-appropriate time-out or taking away privileges.

If you provide a good example, a three- or four-year-old child is capable of mimicking your behavior and acting like a proper little adult at times, but don't get confused by thinking they have reasoned themselves to this behavior pattern, and that if you just give them the logic they will do the right thing. We should always speak words of reason to our children, because we are training and want to associate good reasoning and good decision making. At this point, we are laying the foundation for a good decision-making system in our child's head.

The proper conclusion to this is to take notice of what associations you are making as a parent. Are you ignoring or even rewarding inappropriate behavior? Then you are wiring the brain that way. Stop it! Do you think it's cute that little Buster can talk back? Be very careful, because if that is how you wire his brain, you will likely be the one bearing the brunt of his talking back in a few years, and you along with your child will experience unnecessary pain.

To vary this scenario, let's imagine the meltdown temper tantrum happens at home, and you can be home all day. Another approach is to simply let Buster lay on the floor and scream. You don't need to pinch him because the point is to help him understand what kind of behavior is appropriate and productive, and there are multiple ways to help him learn this. Ignoring screaming is a great way to handle this, if you don't mind the sound and have the time. Buster will learn that screaming gets him nothing and will eventually give up.

Each of us has to be realistic about this in understanding our own capabilities. All of us have different thresholds for what we can endure. If a child screaming makes you tense and upset and drives you toward reacting in anger (reacting in anger is not appropriate) then use the pinch or some similar appropriate and immediate unpleasant consequence.

Note that putting Buster in a corner at this age is not appropriate. His attention spans are short, and a lengthy discipline is wasted in terms of his learning capability. Make your discipline short, to the point, and supported with spoken reasons. Although a young child may not understand these reasons, always explaining why you are disciplining Buster will build understanding over time.

Remember that a major goal at this time in their lives is safety. Good discipline is involved in teaching our kids to work with us to keep themselves safe through appropriate and effective behavioral choices.

You may be asking, What if my child intentionally says no?

The moment will come with most of our kids when they look us in the eye and say, "No!" They know what we want, and they are choosing not to do it. They are not reacting from out-of-control emotions; rather, they are well aware of what they are doing. At first glance, this may not seem to be a safety issue. You may think this is outright disrespect or rebellion. With young children, I am going to ask you to take another perspective. Consider that your child is essentially asking who is in control. They are asking, "Do I get to make the decisions? Am I in charge?"

Is it appropriate for a four year old to be making his or her own decisions without parental direction and supervision? Absolutely not! This is a safety issue. In their stage of brain development, they are not capable of making consistent safe choices.

If we do not respond appropriately here as parents who are in control, we will put our child in an unsafe situation. The reality is Followers are not capable of being in control and their defiant behavior is essentially a request for someone to be in control. I contend that something about our children senses that being uncontrolled is not safe, and they keep pushing to try and find someone to stand up to them and keep them safe. Some children will push at the limits to find out where they are and how certain those limits are.

Do not disappoint your children! Respond to their challenge as parents who are in control. I find that many parents misunderstand this. Instead of showing their young child firmly who is in control, they act surprised by this behavior and get confused as to what to do.

My sister worked as a nurse and often dealt with children and parents. She was amazed at how many times a parent would say, "I can't get Buster to take his medicine." By allowing the child to be in control, parents literally put their child in an unsafe situation, as they weren't taking the medicine they needed. My sister would clarify who was the parent in the room and demonstrate for the parents with 100 percent success how you get children to take medicine.

This begins with an attitude that we are the parents and we are in control. If we have an attitude of uncertainty, children may sense this and challenge us. Children can sense something is wrong if there is an adult in the room who does not know if they are in control of themselves and the situation. Therefore, when a child challenges you, take this simply as a request to determine who is in charge. Respond directly and appropriately to this challenge, clearly letting your child know you are in control. Any other response creates an uncertain situation for your child causing them to sense they are not safe.

Please remember in all of this that the word *discipline* comes from the word *disciple,* and the basic meaning of the word is teaching. All discipline should be teaching aimed at helping our kids to become more self-disciplined. If our discipline with children becomes primarily punishment, we've missed a fundamental point of parenting. As parents, our discipline should be based first on teaching and leading, as when a disciple follows his teacher. At times, punishment may be a necessary tool for correction, but it should be far less important in our homes than the kind of discipline that leads and teaches.

Persistence as a Teaching Tool

Far more than pain, we used persistence to train our kids. Persistence was our first resort, and we used it very early in their lives. Our kids learned that we were completely committed to having them do the right things. Bedtime was a great example. Bedtime was important in our home, and we made it at an early regularly scheduled time, knowing our kids needed their sleep. We exercised persistence and sacrificed some of our social desires to give the kids a schedule their little bodies could count on, and that provided the sleep they needed.

The earliest experience with persistence that I clearly remember was when our oldest learned to climb out of his crib. We put him in bed one night, and soon he appeared in the living room, happy as a clam with his accomplishment. We simply told him it was bed time and put him back in bed. After this happened a number of times, I realized I needed to deal with it. For this lesson, we didn't pinch or get upset; we got persistent.

I first needed to make sure he understood he was not to get out of bed after I put him back down to sleep for the night. I knew he understood this, because if I stood in his room, he would lie down and pretend to be asleep. But once I left the room, his desire to get up overwhelmed my instruction, and he would climb out of his crib and return to the living room once again, clam happy. This behavior reflected the brain working normally for this stage of development. The frontal cortex is the part of the brain that specializes in doing something different than what you want or feel, and it is very underdeveloped at this age. Seeing our young children do something different from what we tell them at a young age shouldn't surprise us one bit. The feeling part of the brain gets too excited and overwhelms the deciding part of their brain. In this case, climbing out of the crib was just too exciting even though I had said *don't*.

Next I needed to make sure that the right events were closely and correctly connected, so our son could make the right associations. To get upset when they walk into the living room at night versus being happy when they walk into the living room in the morning can be confusing.

To avoid this, I used persistence in the following way. When he appeared in the living room, I happily intercepted him, picked him up, carried him to his room, put him in bed, told him the reason he needed to stay in bed and get a good night's sleep, turned off the light, and closed the door with me still inside the room. Sure enough, he climbed out. I intercepted, put him back in bed and reminded him that it was bedtime and that he needed to stay in bed. I repeated, he repeated. We repeated a lot. This took quite a long time the first night. He finally stayed in bed and fell asleep. I did not get angry, I did not punish, I was kindly persistent. The next night I came prepared. He repeated, but only a few times. After two nights, he apparently came to believe that I lived in the room, and that was the end of his trying to climb out of his crib.

Let's do the math and calculate the cost of parental training on this one. When I started, I didn't know if I would be spending three days or three months in his room at night. The only thing I knew for sure was that I would be more persistent than he was. In this case, I actually spent one full evening and part of a second not doing anything I wanted or needed to do. In exchange for my sacrifice, I received thousands of evenings in which he stayed in bed when we put him in bed. That was totally worth the investment.

Were we as parents inconvenienced? Absolutely! We had other things we needed and wanted to do. But we were also more committed to making sure the right thing was done than our son was committed to doing what he felt. This is a choice we can make. Please choose to be a stubborn, yet kind, parent for your kid's physical and psychological safety

Feeling Good as a Teaching Tool

One connection we worked very hard to make was the connection between the reward system in the brain and the right behavior. Our kids are naturally supplied with a reward system that feels good when they do something that pleases mom or dad. We worked to respond positively to the right behavior and to let them know that doing the right thing makes us feel good inside.

This association begins extremely early in life in the Filler stage, right after birth. When we smile, and they smile back, and then we get excited, they feel good because the internal reward system in their brain activates. You will see this in your infants: when you get excited over their behavior, they feel good.

As parents, we can have a powerful influence in our children by making sure we notice the right behavior, and by pointing out what they've done, and then letting them know why what they did was good. Let's say, for example, that your child picks up the toys (not completely, of course, and not totally right as an adult would do it, but they are headed in the right direction). You should let them know and say something like, "Look at you! You picked up your toys! That was helpful so no one trips on a toy. Doesn't that make you feel good inside?"

If you do this immediately, affirming the right behavior, the child will feel good inside, and you will wire your child's brain to connect the right behavior with the good feelings that originate in the reward center of their brain. This will help them become better at choosing constructive rather than destructive behavior. This practice of pointing out good behavior, saying how helpful it is, and getting excited or being genuinely thankful for that behavior creates beneficial connections in our children's brains. If we develop this habit early and continue to practice it, it will strengthen our children's ability to choose positive behaviors throughout their growing years.

State Management

There is another important tool called State Management that tends to minimize defiant encounters and behavioral problems in our kids. To understand State Management, we need to keep in mind that our brains are in a constant state of change. We are moving from feeling full to hungry and back to full, from being rested to tired and back to rested, from being excited to calm and back to excited, from being interested to bored, etc. There is a constant change of the chemicals, input signals, output responses, feelings, and thoughts. The brain experts refer to these brain conditions that affect our behavior as "states." Being excited is a state. Being bored is a state. Apathy, interest, sleepiness, sadness, and happiness are all states. And these states are constantly changing.

States are almost like weather in our brains. They are constantly changing throughout the day, sometimes lasting longer or shorter—a shower here, some wind there, some sunshine, at times cloudy, an occasional thunderstorm, warmer or colder and so on. Fortunately, we can influence the weather in our brains!

Most adults actively manage their states every day. We know that we have to get up early enough to get in that cup of coffee, or that early morning walk, or whatever it might take for us to start the day in a positive mood. We do things to increase our chances of having a good start to the day and therefore a good mood. Unfortunately, our children are usually not skilled in influencing their own states and naturally do very little to adjust their own states.

If we are attentive to our children, we will get to know their likely states, when they happen, and what helps us to put them in better states, like being cooperative or interested, or what puts them in worse states, like being uncooperative or bored. If we begin learning how to manage or cooperate with our children's states early in the Follower stage, we will benefit hugely from this skill in the Finder stage (where it is really needed).

I started learning this lesson a long time before I knew anything about how the brain worked. One Saturday morning, I was sitting in the living room working on a project, and my middle daughter was playing five feet away from me. She was about three years old, and I had a pile of stuff on my lap but had left a book that I needed in the next room. I made what I thought was a very reasonable request and asked my daughter to go into the next room, pick up the book, and bring it back to me. I remember being very surprised when she looked right at me and said, "No!"

In fact, what looked like a cloud of defiance passed over her face. I paused for a micro-moment considering my options. This could be a chance for patience, but even that approach can draw lines of conflict. I could discipline through discomfort. But for some reason that day, I decided to try something I had never tried before.

I looked at her and said, "Please touch the table." She looked at me and the table (about six inches away) and reached out and touched it. "Thank you," I said. "Please touch the chair." She walked a couple of feet and touched the chair. "Thank you," I continued. "Please put this book on the table." She walked over and took the book out of my hand and put it on the table. Then I thanked her and gave her my original request. She ran off and did it without hesitation. I sat there amazed.

What had just happened? I hadn't confronted, used power, patience, or discomfort, and yet she happily did exactly what I asked her to do. Later, I would learn that I had just used State Management before I knew anything about State Management and brain development.

When I made my request, she had been engaged in the extremely important childhood task of play. Playing is a far more basic and necessary drive than we often realize. Her body, brain, heart, spirit, and soul were in play mode. I had just made an entirely unreasonable and difficult request from her perspective. She had to immediately drop the state she was in (the play state) and shift to another state (the "let's do something for Dad" state).

One problem we have as parents is that we don't give the play state enough importance. If you look at all mammals, one of the main jobs of youth is play! This desire to play is a natural bent they have that prepares them for the adult world. Whether it's a kitten trying to catch her tail, a young girl playing tag, or a young boy drawing cartoons, these are extremely important and ought to be respected by adults as key developmental activities of children.

Because of the importance of play, I'd like to review and emphasize an earlier example of how important play is for brain development. One area of the brain that is greatly influenced in its development by play is the cerebellum. The cerebellum sits at the back lower part of the head and contains approximately 40 percent of the brain's neurons, yet it is only 10 percent of the brain's volume. This means there is something incredibly important about this part of the brain since it is so packed with brain cells.

One of the functions of the cerebellum is physical coordination. Running, skipping, jumping, rolling over, balancing, tumbling, riding dad as a horsey, getting twirled around, etc., develop this part of the brain. The more you play physically, the more this area develops. Now add to this the discovery scientists have made in the last few decades: this area of the brain not only coordinates your body but it also appears to coordinate the thought traffic or communication between areas of your brain.

So play literally not only makes you more coordinated in your body, but it makes you a better thinker! Medical professionals are finding that people with problems in their cerebellum sometimes show symptoms like Attention Deficit Disorder (ADD). So when you let your kids play, play, play, you are helping not only their coordination, but also their ability to learn and think. Playing is extremely important work for kids, and the playful mood is a state that parents should respect.

When I really thought about what I was asking my daughter to do, I had to admit that changing from one state to another very different state was often difficult for me to do as an adult. I was asking her to immediately drop what she was involved in and perform my request. Have you ever been engaged in listening to someone else's story and the good part of the story is just starting when your child runs up and says, "I want a drink"? That is a perfectly legitimate request on the child's part. How do we respond? Usually we response by saying, "Not now" or "Wait a minute." We think this response makes perfect sense. Why can't we immediately shift gears and happily run off and get water? Because we are engrossed in the story. We are in a sitting, listening, interested state. We are not in a "get up and get water" state. If it takes time for us as adults to shift, it will take longer for our kids to shift. Their brains cannot work as efficiently.

Having a child change their state quickly is a difficult task for them to say the least. Learning to help them take small steps toward changing their states almost worked magic in our house.

I loved this discovery. I began practicing this with my kids from that moment on. Later in life, I would learn from a brain perspective what I was doing. But at this time, I would approach the situation by consistently asking myself, "Is Buster likely to want to do my request?" If not, then I would ask, "What can I do to make his cooperation more likely?"

This is why by the time my daughter was in seventh grade, if you remember the beginning of the book, I would not insist that she go pick up dog poop late at night. At that time of night she was in a relaxed, it's close-to-bed-time state. What I wanted her to do required an active state with a motivation to move around. The next morning she would naturally be in this state because she had to get ready for school. Rather than making my request late at night, I would respect the principles of State Management and discover more about this powerful approach. Confrontation existed in our house, but it was minimized, because my wife and I learned to respect what our kids were engaged in and attempted to match our requests with their states, or to influence their states to match our requests.

In many ways, this is a timing issue. There are times of the day when your kids are up and moving around, and that is a good time to ask them to do things that require physical activity. There are times when they are shifting gears between activities. This is a much better time to intervene with a request. They are already in a shifting gear mode, rather than in the middle of an activity.

Admittedly, my tendency is to be selfish in my requests. I want what I want, and I want it now! I see something that needs to be done and without consideration of what my kids are involved in, I drop the request on them. This approach on my part ignores their state and good timing and is a natural way to create conflict.

Not only did we learn to time our requests, but we also learned to influence the states in our kids' heads. For example, I started to ask them to do things that they wanted to do, were super easy to do, were rewarding to do, and that they would be willing to do. The point of this was to create a sense in their minds that my requests weren't always difficult or inconvenient. My requests could even be fun and rewarding.

Sometimes, we as parents can be guilty of telling our kids to do something nearly every time we open our mouths. This can create an "uh-oh" state in our kids toward us. They begin to associate us with always being told to do inconvenient things, and we inadvertently create an unreceptive state. Many of us can identify with this situation as kids. We learned that if we could make ourselves scarce, we wouldn't get asked to do things by our parents.

Mixing up my requests to include plenty of fun requests put them in a more receptive state when I made a request. My wife and I began to make sure that some of our requests were easy to do and fun to do. "Please take this quarter and put it in your piggy bank." We could see the response on their faces. "Really? You're asking me to take a quarter?" "Please drink this hot chocolate." Our children's associations in their heads began to indicate that sometimes our requests were fun, sometimes boring, sometimes easy, and sometimes hard. We worked to avoid all our requests being difficult or inconvenient.

We also learned to help them manage their states by preparing them for our requests. When it was getting close to bed time, we would tell them that in five minutes it will be time to get ready for bed...remember in one minute it will be time to get ready for bed...okay, it's time. Or when the video ends, I want you to...etc.

I should point out that the use of a length of time to help kids prepare for a change is a skill they need to be taught. To say that in five minutes it will be time to get ready for bed tells a young child very little until they learn through experience how long five minutes is. When we first begin to talk about time and use it to help our kids shift gears, we have to teach them a sense of time. If I say, "In five minutes, it's bed time," I should assume they have no sense of what that means. To help, I can come back at three minutes and say, "Now it's three minutes, and you should start putting your toys away" (they don't know how long it will take them to do the various parts of their task, and we have to help them manage their time). "Now, it's one minute, so put your truck in the toy box, your crayons in the desk, your paper on the desk, and get your jammies" (I would be very specific to help them get organized to finish within the five-minute period). If we help our young children like this, they will gain a sense of what five minutes means. This will be extremely helpful to our kids in kindergarten when their teacher says they have five minutes to complete an assignment.

It is no use to anyone to give our young kids a time limit and then get frustrated because they do not complete their task. Teaching a sense of time and helping them monitor their activity is a necessary component of State Management. Other components are, as I have pointed out, to be aware of their current state, think of what state they need to be in, and then either help them move toward the right state or time the request to match a compatible state.

In using state management, did we still experience conflict in our family? Absolutely. We did not escape children whining, blaming, and resisting. We did not escape being tired, grouchy, thoughtless parents. However, after years of making this a habit, conflict was lessened, and then around middle school age, the brain experts helped me understand and apply state management even more effectively than what I had been doing.

Like any skill, once we begin practicing, we will get better. I am still using this skill now that we are into the Fulfiller stage with our kids. It is extremely helpful. Does it always solve the issue? Not at all. We still need other tools in our parenting tool chest, but realizing that our kids' brains are constantly changing, and learning how to work with these changing states, has been one of the most effective tools for creating cooperation in our kids while promoting good relationships with them throughout the parenting process.

School Readiness

Since school will be one of the major events in the lives of our kids during the Follower stage, it will be helpful to spend some time on school readiness. Most of us think that reading, writing, and arithmetic skills compose the foundation of school readiness. They do not. They can be a *part* of school readiness. In my opinion, it is not the amount of academic information that a kid has acquired before entering school, but the ability of the child to operate successfully in the school environment that constitutes school readiness.

Your child's brain is designed to acquire information. You can't stop it. They naturally love to learn. The biggest problem in many school situations, as Eric Jensen commented in one of his seminars, is that our kids enter kindergarten loving to learn, and we beat this love out of them by the third grade. This is not the school's fault. It is a cooperative problem between the family and the school.

Part of the solution to this problem is being aware of when a child is ready to learn. Although children learn all the time, their capacity to learn and the age at which they learn specific skill sets can vary widely. The ability to read and write is a good example. Unlike speaking, the brain is not naturally wired to read and write. I used to think if one could read, one could write. I have learned since then that different areas of the brain are involved in these processes, and it does not follow that the ability to read means one can write. Some kids may be ready to read but not have the fine motor skills to write.

The same can be said of aspects of drawing. I had assumed that if you were a good freehand artist, you could copy a fairly simple picture, yet I have seen very talented young artists that could not copy a far simpler picture than they could draw free hand. Copying takes skills in knowing where to start, how to break down the picture you are looking at, and then how to take appropriate steps to reproduce it. That is largely an organizational task requiring different skills than freehand drawing.

Added to these individual differences are windows of learning opportunity or sensitive times when a child will more easily pick up a certain skill. We have already discussed one of these in that a child will naturally pick up the sounds of language during the first year of life.

Another set of skills that likely has windows of opportunity is related to musical abilities. Our children had lots of exposure to hearing music and making music from very early in their lives, and we've always had a piano in our home. We were interested to determine about what age we should have our kids take formal piano instruction as opposed to just playing on the piano.

After interviewing a number of music teachers, we found that if we started our child early in formal piano instruction, say at age four, they would likely be no further along at age nine than a child that started at age six or seven. What experience showed these teachers was that for children who started at four and for those who started at six or seven, they were equal in piano playing ability by age nine. This was long before either we or our music teachers had studied anything about brain development and sensitive periods for learning. However, experience and wise teachers had already figured out that learning readiness preceded learning. When a child was ready to learn, the learning would go much more quickly and effectively. So we concluded that, generally, a child could achieve the same piano playing ability in two years or four years, depending on when you started them.

A very important concept to understand is that all children will generally follow the same learning process but at somewhat different rates. By this, I mean that for a child to have neat hand writing, he or she will have to develop fine motor skills. This will depend on how much they practice and when certain areas of their brain come online. That timing will differ to some extent for all kids. If we know that our kids will be developmentally different, then it is important to instill a sense in our children that learning is fun, that everyone learns at different rates, and they will be behind some children in some things, ahead of some children in others, and that's okay.

My wife and I have witnessed parents who are anxious because their children are developmentally behind other children. Developmental differences ought to be the expectation. This anxiety is largely because we as parents are measuring progress on too short a timeline rather than taking the long-run perspective. I would much rather have my middle school child love to learn than have him know more facts than his neighbor. It can be more harmful to your young children to push them academically rather than instilling a love for learning and an understanding that everyone learns differently. This parental perspective will help your child feel valued for who they are and how they learn.

Throughout our children's lives, learning readiness will aided by a sense that learning is enjoyable and beneficial. It is a part of our natural desire as humans to explore, discover, and learn. Too often our kids get burdened with comparisons that show they aren't doing as well as someone else, that they aren't meeting standards, or that they can't perform in the classroom as expected, and they end up feeling incompetent and embarrassed.

This is an incredible barrier to learning being a joy. These kids are learning, but the unfortunate lesson is that learning, at least in the school context, means embarrassment and failure. So like many sensible adults, they will find ways to avoid this negative situation by not participating at school, seeking interests outside of school, becoming a comedian to focus attention off academics, dropping out, or by some other means of avoidance.

The real question, then, is not what can we teach our children before entering school, but how can we help our children keep the love of learning and successfully navigate the school environment?

What brain skills can be established that will make learning acquisition easier? What attitudes can we help them develop to make them more resilient when facing difficult challenges?

A critical part of the solution then is getting our kids ready to function successfully at school. One problem is that many of us don't send kids to school ready to be in an organized learning environment. The schools are too often overloaded with behavior issues, teachers struggle just to maintain classroom order, and learning becomes hit or miss. Many children have more difficulty with successfully participating in the school learning environment than they do learning the material.

One common aspect of all school learning environments involves schedules or routines. On Monday, in Ms. Kendall's class, the children arrive by 8 am, empty their hands and backpacks, put their lunches and coats away, greet their teacher, line up at the door, enter the classroom in an orderly manner, find their chairs, begin the activity on the whiteboard at their desks, etc. On Tuesday, the children arrive at 8 am, empty their hands and backpacks, put their lunches and coats away, greet their teacher, line up at the door, enter the classroom in an orderly manner, find their chair, begin the activity on the whiteboard activity, etc. On Wednesday.... You get the idea. It is extremely helpful by the time our children are entering school to have had routines and schedules as a part of their life.

Some part of our home life, then, ought to have routines just like school has routines. For us, one routine I have already mentioned that we followed religiously was bedtime. On Monday night at seven o'clock we would announce that in ten minutes it would be time to get ready for bed, around 7:05 we would give a reminder, and then around 7:07 we would have the kids put their toys away, go to their rooms, get on their jammies, go to the bathroom, brush their teeth, snuggle in bed, read a story, give kisses, and turn off the light. On Tuesday night at seven o'clock we would announce that in ten minutes…etc.

This is a huge help to kids in getting them ready to operate in an environment where a schedule will need to be followed. Can we vary our schedule? Certainly! They will at school. But schools will vary the schedule for a good reason, and we should do the same and give the reasons for our occasional schedule changes.

If Buster doesn't want to start getting ready for bed at 7:10, we should give him reasons: Sleep is when you grow, and it will help you grow up strong like daddy. We should also give him choices: Would you rather pick up your toys first or brush your teeth first? Either way, he needs to learn that it is time for bed. While he might have a choice of how to get ready for bed, getting ready itself is not a choice. At school, lunch will be at a certain time every day. It doesn't matter if Buster wants to go to lunch or not, it will happen at 11:35 am. It will help Buster (and Buster's teacher) to have Buster learn the skill of following a schedule even when he doesn't want to.

This will also assist Buster in making transitions. Much of a school day is involved in activity, transition, listening, transition, activity, transition, recess, transition, etc. Helping Buster learn to get ready for the next event is a great school readiness skill. Putting your toys away, washing your hands, and sitting at the table while you wait for everyone to arrive and mom to get the food on the table gets you ready for dinner. All of these steps create a transition between playing and eating. Knowing how to go through the transitional steps to get ready for the next activity is a huge school readiness skill.

Having the family sit together for a meal as often as possible then is great school readiness training. First, as we have noted, the children get to practice transitions in getting ready for dinner. Next, they wait at the table while everything is put on the table and everyone arrives (note: this practice of waiting to start dinner together is better for school readiness than everyone digging into the food as they sit down). After starting to eat together, they will sit around the table and learn to take turns telling a story about their day and listening to others. Taking turns is a basic but important school readiness skill. The ability to be quiet and listen is also an important school readiness skill. Even the dinner time request, "Buster, please pass the salt," with a successful response is an important school readiness skill. It is the skill of following directions.

Kids need to know how to follow directions. "Please pass the salt" is a one-step direction. By the time children are five years old, they should be able to follow two- to three-step directions. "Buster, please take the yellow crayon and draw a doggie for Mommy." "Buster, please put your crayons in the crayon box, put the box on the shelf, and go tell your sister it's dinner time." That's a three-step direction. If Buster doesn't succeed, we should not get upset. Buster is a child, this is a skill he doesn't have, and it will take time to learn. However, when he succeeds we should comment, "Way to go, Buster. You put your crayons away and let your sister know it's dinner time. That was very helpful."

Note that I did not say, "Thank you!" Any words of appreciation and positive praise that we give are good, but we can also help our kids by choosing a more appropriate response. "Thank you" implies you did it for me. So if Buster out of his own free will goes and gets me a glass of water, "Thank you, Buster. That is so nice!" is a great response.

If I am asking Buster to do something involving a skill, it is a great teaching tool to review what Buster did, how he was successful, and how that helped. "Buster, you put your toys away. Now no one will trip on them. That was very helpful!" That will help Buster understand that he is not just doing something for me (this is what he might learn if I only say thank you), but he is developing a powerful skill that will help him become successful.

Describing Our Child's World

Notice that describing to Buster what he is accomplishing is a powerful teaching method. This gives us another idea of an activity that we can do that will be huge in getting Buster ready for school. That activity is simply describing to Buster what is happening and what things are. Whenever we are with our young Followers, we should talk to them about what is going on.

"Buster, that's such a nice picture. You used a yellow crayon to make the doggie. That is so pretty." We are teaching colors simply by including description in our comments. "Buster, do you see that doggie? He's wagging his tail. That means he's happy." We are teaching Buster about animal behavior and helping him be safe. "Buster, you look sad. Your face looks like this." Scrunch up your face and watch him take a look. By this, we are teaching Buster about his feelings and how he expresses them. "Buster, thank you for bringing me three rocks. Look here's one, there's two, and this is three." We are teaching Buster numbers by simply being descriptive. "Buster, look at this picture in this book. What do you think this picture is about?" When Buster tells you, respond with something like, "You told a great story about that picture. Let's read the words and see what they say about the picture." In this way, you are telling Buster that pictures have meaning we can learn to understand, and words have meaning we can learn to understand. By doing this we are developing reading readiness.

We should continually talk to our preschoolers, describing the world and activities around them and inviting them to tell us about their world and what they think. Our description and direction is also helpful in social interaction.

When Buster is with playmates, we should regularly take time to be attentive to how they are interacting. When Buster attempts to resolve an issue by yelling or hitting, we should step in and correct that behavior. If Buster calls his friend names, we should help him understand how that hurts feelings and friendships. With friends, Buster needs to learn all the friendship skills such as taking turns, being friendly, resolving problems, apologizing when he does something wrong, knowing when to ask for an adult's help, and understanding what is appropriate when interacting with his friends. This is what we teach as parents by being involved. In all of this we must remember they are children, and that initially they won't do most of these things very well.

If you spend time with your child doing these kinds of activities, you will give your child a school readiness education that few preschools can match.

Earlier, we talked about brain-friendly discipline in terms of helping wire our children's brains in healthy ways. One appropriate addition at this point is to emphasize that when we describe our child's behavior to them, we begin to wire self-understanding. A baby fusses because he is hungry. It is not a given that a three year old will know he is acting fussy because he is hungry. When our kids get hungry and fussy, it is helpful to them to say, "Buster, you're hungry. Fussing does not tell me if you are hungry. Please use words. What you are trying to say is 'I'm hungry.'"

One good illustration from our family that we used early on in this area was when our children began squirming and fussing in their high chairs. My wife knew they wanted down, but she did not immediately put them down. She described their behavior and gave them words. "You're squirming because you want down. Squirming does not get you down. Say, 'Down, please,' and I will put you down." It wasn't long before our very young children learned that squirming and fussing did not get them down, but the words, "Down, please," were very powerful and resulted in them getting down. That was a two-word phrase they all began using very early in life.

This two-word phrase was the beginning of many phrases that they would learn in the same manner. It is a very empowering approach to describe our children's behavior to them, allowing self-understanding of their feelings and behavior, and then to help them use words to accomplish what they want. Using words appropriately will be an extremely powerful method of accomplishing what we want throughout our lives.

Follower Part I – Summing It Up:

We've covered a lot of territory. Let's summarize where we've been before we take on some more areas that are especially helpful in our kids' transition to the Finder years.

- First, we said that the Follower years are in some ways an extension of the Filler years. In other words, the areas of the brain that begin working in the Filler years keep on working, but now more areas of the brain come online. This means that a lot of learning will still be implicit, but the new areas coming online mean that our children will cooperate with our teaching and our example, and we will have a tremendous amount of influence. The mirror neurons encourage our kids to copy us, and factors such as bonding through oxytocin will continue to work, meaning that our kids will have a natural desire to follow our example. Therefore, we need to be present and involved.

- Next, we said we can increase our effectiveness in helping our kids grow and mature if we understand some other important ideas.

  o One idea is that in some ways we contribute to the wiring of our children's brains. This started even before birth, and in the Filler years we helped direct connections by controlling our children's environment and by interacting with them. In the Follower years, we will have a chance to help wire the part of their brain that handles decision making and thinking about future consequences. Our wise use of praise, persistence, teaching, and discipline can help connect their brains in such as way that their feelings don't control them,

and by doing this we provide our children greater freedom
and ability to make good choices.

o   Along with this, we looked at State Management. This is
an incredibly helpful tool to learn and practice during the
Follower years. It will benefit us tremendously throughout
the rest of our parenting. The idea of State Management
is to watch what kind of a state or disposition our child is
in. Then we can learn to time our requests to match their
disposition or influence their disposition to match our
requests. This tool, learned well during the Follower years,
will be incredibly valuable during the Finder years. It is not
only excellent for helping our kids behave in ways we think
are more productive, but it helps us as parents behave in
more productive ways. We found that understanding our
kids' states changed our behavior as parents for the better. It
is difficult to say whether using state management affected
our parental behavior or the kids' behavior more. All we
know is that it is extremely helpful.

o   Then we looked at school readiness. School readiness is
not sending your children to school with their heads full
of academic facts and capabilities. School readiness is more
about preparing them to learn in an organized environment.
Remember, we said they will learn, and we can't stop
that process. What often gets in the way is not that they
don't know enough, but that they get into conflict with a
school environment or become discouraged or embarrassed
by the school environment. We can help this by having
schedules at home, and teaching them to make transitions,

to follow directions, to know how to wait their turn, to make requests, and to attend to basics such as knowing how to blow their nose.

o Finally we said helpful information can be given to our kids by describing their world to them as we experience life together. This description includes not only the outside world, but helping them put words to their inner world, their own feelings. We also give needed direction to our kids when we help them interact socially with friends.

One way to think about our children's needs during this time is in terms of safety. In the Filler years, we create a place of safety that protects our kids. In the Follower years, we become a place of safety that provides teaching, direction, and appropriate limits that help them navigate their world. In the Filler years, we largely keep them from dangerous places. In the Follower years, we teach them to explore potentially dangerous places safely (crossing the street, riding a horse) and then monitor them as they take on these activities.

As parents we provide acceptance, protection, support, and direction, and a place that they can always run to when needed. By supervising their exploration into the world, we meet one of the brain's most basic needs of safety, and brains that feel safe learn better.

Chapter 6

Follower Part II

In the last chapter, we finished with the idea of providing safety for our children as they explore the world. I want to expand on that idea by discussing healthy enrichment through exploration. In the early Follower years, our nest should begin to change from a safe place that limits what our children are exposed to into a safe place from which our children can explore. Studies with monkeys show that a devoted mother who attends to her infant's needs produces a more secure infant that shows more confidence in exploring his or her environment. Mom still provides the safe place to run to if a situation seems uncertain. A good mom will also monitor these explorations and step in when necessary to direct or protect the young monkey.

In the same way, if we have provided a safe place for our children, their natural response will be to use us as a safe base from which to explore. In cooperation with this desire, we can direct that exploration in ways that benefit our child. This is a natural process that enriches our children's experience and encourages healthy brain development.

Enriching Experiences

It is important to understand how these enriching experiences work. Research has been done with animals to discover how they learn, and as a result of how they learn, how smart they become. One of my favorite research stories, told by Dr. Robert Sapolsky in his course on Biology and Human Behavior, has to do with genius mice and not-so-genius mice that were created through genetic engineering.[9]

Researchers discovered a gene that was linked to how quickly mice could learn. By manipulating this gene, they produced mice that were quick learners. They gave these mice the equivalent of a mouse IQ test and proved they were little geniuses. This, of course, was incredibly exciting to the scientists, as they had just produced evidence that aspects of how smart we are have a genetic component. This is what we all have suspected, since it seems that smart parents often have smart kids.

In other words, this gave evidence that we're smart because of the genes mom and dad gave us. To further support their conclusion, they knocked out (deactivated) the smart gene in another group of mice and produced a bunch of mice that were IQ challenged. These guys did not do well on their mouse IQ tests.

At this point, the scientists had a great story. Supply this gene and the mouse is smart, take away the gene and the mouse is dumb.

What more proof do we need that intelligence is determined by genetics?

But because these were really smart scientists, they took the experiment one more step. They asked the question, "What would happen if we put the 'dumb' mice in an enriching environment that encourages learning?" So they did that experiment and were amazed by the results.

The mice with the dumb genetics became just as smart as the smart mice over time. Now their great and simple story was still great but not as simple. It appears that being smart is not just a product of our genes but of our environment as well. Yes, the genes we get from mom and dad can influence our capabilities, but so does our experience. We cannot change the specific genes we give to our kids, but we can influence their experience. By influencing their experience, we change a lot of things, and research shows we are even influencing the genes we gave them to perform differently. So what is an enriched environment, and how can we help our kids benefit from that kind of environment?

One of the common misconceptions is that an enriched learning environment is a spectacular, jam-packed life crammed full of academic experiences. From 8 to 2:30 we go to kindergarten, then from 2:30 to 5:30 we go to Harvard Prep Daycare, and after dinner we do math and reading worksheets. Believe it or not, this is likely *not* an enriching environment at all. The primary reason is that this kind of environment does not usually provide contrast. Contrast is very important for enrichment. Many academic environments and academically oriented parents simply provide more of the same.

We observed this repeated academic environment through friends' children when we lived in Japan. It was very common for grade school kids to go to school during the day, then go to Juku after school, then come home and eat a late dinner and sit down and do homework until midnight. Juku was like a school on steroids where the kids received supplemental academic education. They did this every day of the week and usually had homework to the max on the weekends.

As educators, my wife and I both knew that Japan was having success in teaching kids to do well on tests. We also knew from living and teaching there that something was amiss in the Japanese educational system. Our perspective was that life is not primarily about taking tests. They are only a small part of life. The decision for schools and countries to "teach to a test" is fraught with danger, and while it should be a goal, it should not be the primary goal. Our experience as teachers in Japan was that while our students could take tests, they were not as creative and inventive in problem solving as American students who might have been less skilled in test taking. It is my conviction that success in learning, and enrichment that encourages brain development, is much more than taking tests. Let's take a moment to look at what research is telling us about enrichment and learning. In his book *Enrichment and Learning* Eric Jensen summarizes this research nicely.[10]

Researchers have taken animals (mainly rats and mice) and put them in various environments in experimental studies. Examples of the environments are as follows. Some environments were spartan, with only the basics of food and water. Some environments were social and had buddies along with the food and water. Some environments were enriched with toys, changed daily, along with buddies. Some environments were pools forcing the rats to swim (which they don't like). Some provided wheels to run on (which they love). Other environments had purposeful versus non-purposeful activity, in which the activity was the same but was either linked to meaning or not linked to meaning (for example, if the rat received food as a reward from an activity, that would make it "meaningful"). The researchers in these various projects then evaluated the effects of these different situations on the learning and brain development of the various animals involved.

Here are some of their findings. Environments that included exercise rats liked (for example, rats love running on wheels) produced a greater number of new brain cells than in rats that didn't exercise. Animals in enriched environments kept more of their new brain cells than animals in any other environment. In fact, animals in enriched environments had brains that developed more volume and thickness in certain beneficial areas. So did animals in purposeful environments. Animals in stressed environments could actually lose brain cells, and animals in exercise environments where they didn't like the exercise (in this case, rats swimming— they don't like water) didn't produce any more new brain cells than couch potato rats that sat around all day.

What have researchers generally seen through these experiments? Exercise that animals like is really good for producing new brain cells. However, if the animals don't use the new brain cells, the brain cells die. So animals in an enriched environment where they have contrasting situations and face new learning opportunities retain more of the new brain cells produced and their brains develop more. Animals with buddies produce and keep more brain cells than animals without buddies. Animals who are stressed can actually lose brain cells. Animals that exercise and are stressed aren't any better off than animals that don't exercise and aren't stressed.

Now, you can't just assume that because something works in an animal like a rat that it works the same way in humans. However, researchers are finding some of these same effects in monkeys, and are also finding evidence that these effects are true in humans.

It is important, then, to understand what enriched and meaningful environments are, and how we might provide these for our kids. One of the most important aspects of enriched environments is contrast. In other words, more of the same, even lights flashing, spectacular stuff, is not inherently enriching. So going from school where you do math worksheets, to Juku where you do math worksheets, to home where you do math worksheets for homework is not the best environment for the brain. This also means that allowing our kids and ourselves to do only the things we already know and are comfortable with is not the best environment for the brain. We should be taking on new learning challenges and explore novel situations.

We should not do this in ways that are overly stressful to us (*Come on! Jump out of the plane! It's good for your brain!*), but in incremental ways that mildly stress us (*Let's sign up for choir. It's something new and different*), and allow us to make progress. What is hugely stressful and what is a healthy challenge vary with the individual. This is why it is important for parents to consider each child and their need to be appropriately challenged.

So what does this mean for our kids? First, I will remind you that they need to play, to run and jump and imagine and pretend. This time is incredibly valuable for brain development. Kids need recess or physical activity times. Teachers ought to think twice about ever keeping kids inside during recess as a discipline measure. The activity at recess or during physical education reduces kids' stress, provides exercise that produces all sorts of brain enriching and protecting chemicals, and encourages the birth of new neurons, which can increase learning.

Next, provide contrast. My wife was a genius at this. She knew that kids need times of boisterous fun and times of quiet. Times with friends and times alone with their thoughts. Times of creative reconstruction of the house into castles and forts, and times of putting everything away and restoring order. They need to rearrange their room and see if they like it better.

They need to tell stories, hear stories, make up stories from pictures, write stories with scribbles, write stories with words, act out stories, tell puppet stories, direct stories, act in stories, imagine stories, and create stories with siblings taking turns giving one word at a time (a great improvisation exercise to develop quick and innovative thinking). Kids love to tell or act out these stories when we as parents take time to be their audience.

They need to go outside with mom and walk around the block during the spring, then during the summer to find changes, then the fall to see more changes, then the winter. They need to do this at the local park, then maybe on a hike.

They need to go outside with friends or play inside with friends and begin to navigate their own social worlds. They need to know others have feelings as they do. They need to learn to take turns. They need to know how to go first and feel privileged, or to allow another to go first and feel generous and happy inside. They need supervision, help, mediation, and direction in these social relationships. They need to have a sleepover inside and, if possible, outside.

They need to hear why things are important. Why math helps you buy something you want. Why reading can open up new worlds of imagination. Why sleep helps you grow. Why pets need to be cared for every day. Why we obey our parents. Why cooperation is important. Why some things feel really hard and why some things feel really soft.

They need help to know what new things to experience. What new opportunities they can try. What stretches their abilities without stretching them too much. If they stretch too much and fail, they need to know that all of us try again when we fail, and failing helps us to do better the next time. They need to know that failing is actually a good thing because we learn by failing. They need our confidence, our assurance, our praise, and our loving arms as they try new things.

They need someone who listens to their teacher and finds out where they need help, or what specific skills they need to develop. If they can't learn letters at school because they have a difficult time sitting in a chair and learning, they need someone to write the letters on the floor and jump on each one, yelling it out. They need to jump from letter to letter until they can spell cat, mat, and bat. They need to play "find the letters of the alphabet" in the signs you pass when you go out driving or ride the bus.

They might need help with numbers. They need to learn to get two eggs for the cake, to add one cup of flour and three tablespoons of sugar, and put ten sprinkles on top of each cupcake. They need to jump down the stairs and count each one as they go and tell you how many stairs there are. They need to look at the clock and tell you when it is three o'clock, because when it is three o'clock they get a snack. They need to count to ten because after they say ten, they open their eyes and start another game of hide and go seek.

They need to play Candy Land, Go Fish, Chutes and Ladders, and other board games. They need to know how to move five spaces, pick up the yellow card, and follow the directions on the card. They need to see that waiting to let Charis and Amy take turns results in a fun game. They need to sometimes win and sometimes lose. They need to play charades, capture the flag, and soccer.

They need to draw using different colors and textures such as chalk, or crayons, or pencils. They need to make big drawings on the sidewalk and small drawings on the back of their hand.

All of this can be very enriching to our children, and I want you to notice that in implementing these activities, we've spent very little money. Many companies would have you believe that enrichment is buying a noisy, flashing, speaking gizmo, or traveling to Paris. Enrichment is mainly providing contrasting and meaningful experiences for your particular child, and we as parents are the experts on what our child is experiencing and what is likely to provide meaning and contrast for them.

If our kids are not doing well at learning a certain subject in school, review how they are learning. If it is rote memorization, add meaning by showing how the words are important or used in everyday life, or by putting the words in a story or play, or by using them to make a diagnosis or to solve a problem. If they have to sit still all the time, do some of the same school work while running and jumping or shooting baskets. If they are only learning about animals through pictures, take them to the humane society or a pet store or the zoo. If they can't add numbers, take out some M&Ms. When they can tell you how many there are of each color and how many there are in total, they can eat them.

If they are learning about ecosystems from a book, take them to the nearest swamp, park, or stream and catch a frog, then let it go. Talk about what it means for that frog to have a place to live. Compare it with where you live and what you need to live.

If they can't sit quietly and write a sentence, there are ways to help. Have them tell you a sentence and you write it down, then switch and you tell a sentence while they write it down. Whisper the sentence or yell it out. Do it standing, do it jumping, do it being still, do it sitting down. Have them send daddy a text message.

This may sound busy and tiring, but much of this stuff can be done as you go through your day with just a little extra time. You will have to walk stairs, so why not count them at the same time? You will have to shop at the store, why not count the things in the basket as you put them in and take them out? As you drive or ride the bus, have the kids look for letters. As you go down the same street, have your kids tell you how things change with the seasons. As you cook dinner, have kids help. Have your kids buy the bus tickets at the ticket machine.

Then for sanity's sake, take a break. Even though you've turned off that TV, pop in a DVD every now and then, let the kids veg, while you relax or do something different. Let a friend take care of your child. They will see how another family does things and that in itself will be enriching for them and a break for you.

One of our friends taught her kids to give each other lessons based on what they learned in school every day. So every afternoon when the older ones got home from school, they would teach something they learned to the younger kids. This gave Mom a break every afternoon. Another form of a break is to make sure you share your enriching activity approaches with another mom or dad and take turns doing them with the other's children, or do them together.

Goal Setting

If you've followed the advice in this book, you've already started another very important process in working with your child's brain and development. All of the ways in which we cooperate with brain development provide beneficial impacts for our kids, but activities that help develop the frontal cortex will not only benefit our kids as Followers but also have a huge positive impact on the Finder and Fulfiller stages. Remember, the frontal cortex is the part of the brain that can plan ahead, make decisions, and choose to delay immediate responses for future rewards. These abilities are critical for our children's success.

We have already discussed ways to help the frontal cortex develop. Early in our children's lives we can encourage creative and elaborate play. Play in which children take on roles and act out those roles, such as putting on a play for parents with siblings or friends, having a tea party, or pretending to be Luke Skywalker and

Han Solo in destroying the Death Star, are great exercise for the frontal cortex. Board or card games that require children to take turns, follow directions, and think about strategy provide excellent exercise as well.

Also early on, we can help our kids give words to their desires. If they want down, we can teach them to say the words "down, please" and give them the idea that they can have power using words to accomplish things. This requires children to resist the desire to whine and squirm and choose to focus that energy in a more productive activity like asking "down, please." This is a simple way to help develop the frontal cortex of our kids' brains.

We have also discussed giving choices and letting our children work through those choices like deciding what they want to do first in getting ready for bed. This is another great exercise for the frontal cortex. One of the best and most productive ways to extend this frontal cortex development is through goal setting and children are very capable of setting goals.

I remember as a kid that one of my favorite activities was to stage a naval battle on our lawn during the Fourth of July. I was in grade school and had a dad who liked firecrackers. I would work during the summers to earn some money and then begin buying and building model warships. I couldn't afford many, but I would buy what I could, get some for gifts, and build them during the wet, rainy winter months in the state of Washington.

When the Fourth of July got close, Dad would drive us to the Lummi Indian Reservation where I would purchase firecrackers. Fortunately, Dad was a kid at heart in many ways, and he always bought a pretty fair share of them for himself as well. Dad supplied the Fourth of July nighttime show fireworks, and I supplied the fireworks out of my own pocket for the daytime naval battle.

Once I had my firecrackers, I would install them into my ships. Usually on the Fourth, I would arrange my ships into two fleets and begin the battle. The battle consisted of various techniques (like tossing lit fire crackers at the ships) to try and get the ships to blow up.

Now, I realize I am not being politically correct, as many might think my dad was crazy for letting me play with things that explode. Remember also that we lived in the rainy State of Washington and the grass was green, fire possibility was extremely low, and Dad kept a water hose close and a watchful eye on my activities. Please hang on for the point as I am not promoting firecrackers, but activities that require our kids to make choices, plan ahead, and delay gratification.

For a grade school boy, blowing up ships was magical fun. This magical fun had a great brain development side that was not dependent on the fireworks themselves, but on the planning I was doing. This was an age-appropriate exercise in goal setting (again, not the firecrackers but the event planning) that was maybe even a bit beyond my years, but boy, was I motivated! I was setting up a plan for the entire year that involved earning money, saving money, planning purchases, building models, then modifying those models, and putting a production together after the year of planning. This involved my frontal cortex big time.

I had to think about future events, plan ahead, and delay gratification by resisting spending money on things I wanted but that wouldn't get me to my production. I did have to learn some things about safety from Dad, and this put me on a twelve-month planning cycle, because I could only get firecrackers near the Fourth of July.

At this point in my life, my parents weren't working on goal setting with me, as I am going to advise you to do, but giving me opportunity and authority to pursue things like this set in motion the development of goal-setting skills that I still benefit from today. The problem with leaving it up to me without parental direction (I chose fireworks to blow up ships) is that I did give myself some pretty severe burns on my hand one year, and I didn't plan for some very important areas of life in which parental direction would have been a great help.

Where we are headed in learning about goal setting is very important to our kids' welfare. Let me describe the goal and then we will discuss how to get there.

After the Follower years are the Finder years. During the initial Finder years, we will see that in most kids, the brain appears to take a vacation from being sensible and rational (though in reality it does not). I am injecting some humor here, but for brains to develop to the next level, they have no choice but to go through a significant change that can be unnerving to parents. Wouldn't it be fantastic if we were able to implant some general guiding ideas in our kids that would stay with them during these seemingly irrational and impulsive years?

We can! That's the beauty of the Follower years. Remember, I have said that during these years, most of our kids are naturally designed to follow us and our ideas, if we are present and involved in their lives. By building goal-setting skills and introducing goal-setting topics and exercises, we can help them set some very important guiding lights for when the lights seem to go out in their heads during adolescence.

One of the exercises I use with grade school kids goes something like this:

I begin with a discussion of brain development using brain scans and show them the effect that bad decisions, such as smoking, can have on the brain. Smoking is the leading behavioral cause of strokes. Most fifth graders will see right through any positives they've heard about smoking and do a very good job of listing the reasons why smoking is bad. We agree that starting to smoke is a bad decision.

I then show them a graph which estimates the age at which people start to smoke. It peaks at about age fifteen or sixteen. We discuss the graph and show how it peaks and then goes to nearly zero by age twenty-five. This leads to a discussion about why we tend to make bad decisions when we are age fifteen and sixteen, and why decision-making continues to improve through age twenty-five. I then invert the smoking graph and call it a good decision graph. Good decision making hits a low about age fifteen or sixteen.

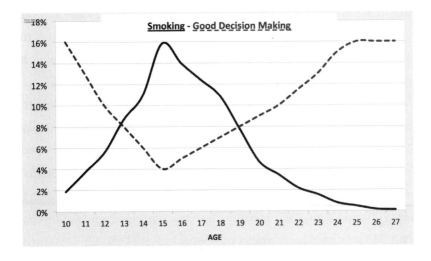

Kids understand this pretty well, and then we discuss the good changes coming in brain development and how that can include bad decision making and why. Changes always lead to new ways of doing things, and learning new things is always accompanied by mistakes. Mistakes are how we learn. However, I tell the kids, by preparing for the coming changes, we can help our mistakes not result in bad decisions with long-term consequences. This leads to a talk about our frontal cortex and exercising it to make good decisions. We then use not smoking as an example of a goal we can set now, when our brains are working well, that will keep us from taking up a damaging habit when we are sixteen.

If done appropriately, in good open discussion with honest facts and figures, the kids will likely adopt a goal of not smoking as their own decision. This is key. One of the characteristics of the Finder years is that brain development pushes them to begin making decisions for themselves. We will find out more about why their brains are wired this way in the next chapter. We have to realize that if we try and make these decisions for our kids in the Finder years (*You can't smoke! Over my dead body, young man!*), there is a part of their brain that comes online and motivates them to come to a decision different than ours. But if the decision not to smoke is one that they made during the Follower years, they are far more likely to see the decision as their own and maintain it through the coming changes.

This exercise then leads the whole group into a goal-setting exercise in which we talk about goals and write down goals for many areas of their lives. One method I use is a worksheet called the *One Page Miracle* that comes from a course for kids that Dr. Daniel Amen created on brain development.[11] This worksheet encourages kids to set goals for work or earning money; for their body, mind, and spirit; and for relationships with parents, siblings, and friends.

I then help them use this to do a frontal cortex exercise. I ask the students to keep the written goals somewhere where they can see them every day and then do the following. Read the goal and ask yourself this question. "Did my behavior today (or this week) get me closer to or further away from my goal?"

Let's say a goal is a better relationship with parents (a common goal even among my "worst" middle school students). They can begin the process of having a goal, reflecting on their behavior, evaluating that behavior, and making adjustments. Some of their goals will be very specific and involve us working with them to identify the steps and time needed to reach their goal.

Understanding how helpful goal setting is explains why organizations such as the Boy Scouts are so wonderful. In Scouts boys can identify a badge they wish to obtain, find help from leaders in how to attain that badge, and make and follow a plan.

The more our kids do this kind of activity through the Follower years, the more capable their brains will be of both making better decisions and of remembering the decisions they've already made through the Finder years. This is huge! In fact I don't feel I can adequately impress you how important this is.

My wife and I hadn't figured this all out during our kids' grade school years, but fortunately, as a family we worked through a book called *Don't Date Naked* during the grade school years. This book had a workbook that led us through goal-setting exercises in the areas of relationships, dating, and sex. As we did this, I sometimes wondered if our kids were too young, but I've found in retrospect that the timing was perfect and any later may have been too late.

Part of the motivation to have this conversation early in our kids' lives came from my own experience. Because of a sexual abuse situation in my life as a very young child and the easy availability of pornography, I usually describe my situation as having essentially started life as a "pre-vert," then through pornography having become a young pervert, and being well on my way to becoming a "pro-vert" by sixth grade. However, one speech changed all this.

It was an ordinary school day about halfway through the morning. So far I had spent a significant portion of the day in my sixth grade classroom watching Lauren sit on Wesley's lap and kiss. I was thinking that this seemed exciting, and I should start giving it a try. Believe it or not, the teacher was in the room, but he had given us a curtained off area of privacy where we, as young adults, could go and do responsible school things.

So Wesley was apparently responsibly kissing Lauren and a bunch of us were responsibly gathered around taking notes. I suppose that the sounds gave us away. Despite his assurances of our privacy, I remember Mr. Moore's rather large nose appearing over the top of the curtain, and his eyes beading down on us. He saw what we considered a wondrous scene of Wesley and Lauren in lip lock with us as an intent and approving gallery.

The curtain came down, and a lecture descended. Actually, Mr. Moore was a pretty cool guy, so I listened. Mr. Moore had no idea what he did for me that day.

To realize the impact of his talk, you need to understand that my family raised purebred Norwegian Elkhounds. One of my jobs was intercepting male interlopers and defending our girl from mating with mutts when she was in heat. If she mated with a mutt, our puppies wouldn't be purebred, and we couldn't sell them. So I spent many a night chasing away dogs, repairing our fence, checking on the gates, and keeping track of Thora. I wasn't always successful and had more than once caught a dog in the act or just after the act. These hot-to-trot male dogs were a pain in the butt for me.

Mr. Moore started his speech saying we were more than dogs sniffing around for the next female to mate with, and that meaningful and worthwhile love between two people involved so much more than sex. He went on with further explanation which I don't remember, but I remember totally understanding the sniffing dogs imagery and, no, I did not wish to be in that category. I did some mental goal setting that morning that redirected me from following in Wesley and Lauren's footsteps.

I decided I did not want to behave like a dog in heat and wanted more than that for my life and relationships. I set a goal; a goal that I stood by through high school and college, until my wedding night. I am thankful for Mr. Moore's speech, and the fact that I cannot tell you what it is like to be a pervert, because my direction changed that day, and I began to retreat from my pervert path. I do know I haven't missed a thing. The key aspect to understand in this example is to realize that the reasons Mr. Moore gave in his speech became my basis for a decision during the Follower years. I was a reasonably clear-thinking sixth grader, and I took his information and made my own decision for this area of my life.

Because of this experience, I had an internal sense and felt strongly that we should be talking openly and honestly to our young kids about issues like dating and sex. So our kids entered the Finder years already having thought about many of these issues, and what they might do about them. Since then I have learned that the Follower years are the years to talk openly about sex, drugs, relationships, and all other major issues in life.

How do we get our kids from here to there? *Here* being our kids asking "Down, please" and *there* being our kids thinking something like, "I've thought through this smoking thing and decided it's best not to start. I know the offer will come. When my friends offer me a cigarette, I'm going to simply say that's not for me. If they push, I'll offer other alternatives or push back, and if necessary I will distance myself. I don't want to get hooked, endanger my health, and look forty-five years old when I am thirty-five."

Or to have them make the decision, "I'd really like to skip the unplanned pregnancy thing, the sexually transmitted disease thing, and the getting confused about what love really is thing. I'd like to understand in spirit, soul, and body what it is to commit myself to one person and to work for and be able to celebrate a love that lasts a lifetime."

These are great goals. I realize that we don't always have control whether our goals work out perfectly, but unless we learn to set goals and work to understand how to achieve them, we don't have much chance of getting close. Traveling from here to there will require us as parents to talk to our kids about all the important issues of life. It will also require us to create goal-setting opportunities. Our kids will have wants of various kinds that they will desire. As parents we should pick up on some of these wants and turn them into goal-setting exercises.

Let's say the kids want a dog or a cat, and your situation is amenable to getting a pet. This would be a good time to sit down with the kids and say what a good goal this is, and how you are going to work together as a family to see what it takes to get and care for a pet. I don't want to stifle spontaneity, but a pet is a living, breathing, feeling animal, and we as families should be prepared for what owning a pet requires.

One of the most important aspects of getting a pet is caring for the pet after it arrives. A dog or cat takes attentive care, unpredictable things will happen, and it makes sense to turn this into a good goal-setting exercise.

First, get the kids to consider what they think it will take to get a pet and take care of a pet. Let them know that having a pet is a responsibility, and that we have to learn skills to take care of a pet. If mom and dad are willing to supply the budget, that is great, but you should still talk about how much a pet will cost. Next, what kind of a pet? Help your kids learn a bit about the differences between different kinds of dogs, for example. Then the critical one, what does it take to take care of a pet? Make a list. Who's going to do what? In our house, pets were the kids' responsibility with parental supervision.

We didn't do this next step, but in retrospect, I would get a stuffed dog and name him Barky or something like that. The deal with the kids would be that when we demonstrate we can take care of Barky, we can have a pet. We have a responsibility, not just to dream what we want to have, but to find out what it takes to get and take care of that dream. So set a goal that they have to take care of Barky for a certain amount of time to show that they've learned how to care for a pet.

The kids can do research to find out what it takes to care for a pet. Have them interview you, Grandma and Grandpa, or neighbors with pets about pet care. Have them do some reading. Then begin to practice feeding Barky, watering Barky, taking Barky for walks, letting Barky out to go to the bathroom, cleaning up after Barky has shredded a newspaper all over, searching for Barky when one of the kids leaves the front door or gate open (make this a treasure hunt type event), flea treating Barky, having Barky get upset and scared when there is a thunderstorm, having Barky need to be taken to the hospital when they haven't watered him for three days, cleaning up after Barky has piddled in the middle of the floor or worse (finally a practical application for the plastic poop piles you get at the gag store), and dealing with what happens if Barky gets sick and dies.

You might think this last exercise is morbid, but good goal-setting tries to think about all the issues and possibilities. A significant number of animals have a bad reaction to the anesthesia used for spaying, for example. Animals get hit by cars. You can take this exercise as far you want and, except for the dying conversation (which is important), have as much fun as you want.

Then the day will come when the kids have done all the Barky chores for two weeks straight without a reminder and without a miss. It is now time to replace Barky with the real thing. At this point, we should revisit our list and ask the kids if they think it is complete. We can review what skills we had to learn, what has been the most difficult, what we need to do to keep from making mistakes, and revisit what we think is important to do in having in a pet, and who is responsible for what jobs.

Everyone will be beyond excited as the family travels to the Barky replacement store, pound, or local Humane Society. Hopefully mom and dad have had the forethought of going and prescreening the choices. Kids tend to fall passionately in love with whatever wonderful or sorry thing they see first. So to prevent kids from having a major meltdown because they can't bring Gonzor the cute little puppy pit bull home, make sure you've limited the choices to animals that are likely to work for your family.

Once the puppy or kitten arrives, this scenario takes a life of its own. For a good goal-setting exercise, please keep track of what happens. You need to plan a couple of family meetings to compare what you thought was going to happen to what really is happening. This gives a chance to talk about how well you predicted what would happen, which is a huge goal-setting skill. You can also list what changes you've had to make for the real pet.

This exercise turned a desire into a plan, practiced the plan, experienced what really happened, and compared the actual experience to what was expected. This is a huge help to your child's frontal cortex. You helped your children identify any new skills necessary, and everyone practiced them to get an idea of what is really required. Then you implemented the plan, and reviewed how well you did in planning and predicting what was needed versus what really was needed and what really happened. You can then even discuss how you as a family could have planned better.

That would be a great goal-setting exercise with plenty of natural interest and energy on the kids' part. Note that we could have just driven out the first day and gotten a pet. That is not bad to do, but if we never turn kids' desires into goal-setting exercises like this, think of what we miss in terms of healthy brain development. Let's go through another example quickly to see how another goal-setting exercise might differ.

The day will come when Buster says, "I want a Green Interlaced Zapper with Modulated Operation (GIZMO)." Rather than just forking out the money or pulling out the credit card, tell Buster that is a great goal, and you want to work with him to make that happen.

Let's say a GIZMO costs $9.99. Sit down with Buster and review the cost, how much money he has, how much he can make, and how long it will take.

In our house, we felt strongly that the kids should get an allowance. Our idea was that we are a part of communities throughout life: our families, churches, neighborhoods, etc. As part of a community, we have privileges or resources we have access to, and responsibilities we need to take care of. Our allowance was related to the kids sharing in the community privileges/resources and responsibilities. Our message, then, was that this is money you don't work for, but this is money you receive for being a part of the Doughty family. It's not because you are a good Doughty family member, or a bad Doughty family member; it is yours because you are a part of this family.

We separated this money-sharing aspect from getting paid for chores. Rather than being paid for basic chores, we told them that as a part of the Doughty family there are also ways in which you contribute. They all had things they needed to do. We wanted our kids to learn that no matter what community you are a part of, you should contribute whether you get paid or not, and you will receive benefits from being a contributing member of the community. These benefits are usually not in the form of monetary payment.

They could also do other specific chores for money. We had a list of things they could do that showed how much they would get paid. So in our family, Buster could do some planning. If I just use my allowance, it will take me five weeks (an eternity for a kid) to get my GIZMO, and I can't buy anything in the meantime. However, if I work and do these chores, I can get this in two weeks.

So make the plan with Buster. Then let Buster be in charge of his plan, not you. What this means is that Buster will be in the store and see some toy that he saw on TV and want to buy it. He has the money. It's $4, and he has that amount saved. Resist the temptation as a parent to force him to make his goal. He might buy the $4 item to your disappointment. If so, he will get to day he planned to buy his GIZMO and find he does not have the money.

Now kids are funny. Some kids will be sad and realize they made a mistake and will figure out how to make up for the money they spent. You will feel like a brilliant parent for teaching responsibility. Other kids will say, "I didn't want it anyway." Don't get upset. Just make sure you have the conversation to review what the child planned for, what he did, and how it worked out. Sometimes, it will take many repetitions before a child learns from these exercises.

The idea here is the same: turn a desire into a plan, think of the details to making it happen, and how long it will take. Have Buster implement the plan and review how it goes. Going through this kind of exercise a number of times will prepare you to have conversations about setting goals for very important life matters such as relationships, school, work, and their own body, mind, and spirit. This will allow you to talk about issues such as smoking, having positive friends, getting ready for a good job or college, avoiding drugs, how to navigate through a society that has confused sexual values, etc. Your goal, by the time your child is in fifth or sixth grade, is to have discussed all of the significant issues that will face them in the coming years on their path to adulthood.

The conversation about sex is one that should take place all through the Follower years. Is it appropriate to talk to a kindergartener about sex? Absolutely. The Follower years are the best years to talk about sex, and we ought to take advantage of all the opportunities and questions that come up and be very open and straightforward.

We live in a very wealthy nation and sometimes don't realize what that has done both for us and to us. Most of us have grown up sleeping in a separate room from our parents. This requires a wealthy society. I remember when we lived in Japan, finding out from our friends that the entire family slept in the same room at night (places to live in Japan were generally small and expensive).

So the conversation naturally lead to the question, What did your parents do when they wanted to have sex?

"They had it right in the room with the entire family present," was the reply.

"What did you do?" we asked.

"We were quiet," they answered.

Sex was likely not a mystery in that family.

Those kids' earliest memories of sex were of a passionate physical relationship between their mom and dad in the context of love and commitment that resulted in the miracle of their birth. What better introduction could you have to sex? Is this age appropriate? Absolutely. My advice is, by all means, start the conversation early, and even better, never stop the conversation. Sex is how your children were created, and they should learn from the earliest years about the wonder of their creation. In our own case, we videotaped our kids' births showing them popping out of mommy's bottom, and they could watch that whenever they wanted.

Obviously, you don't need to tell a four year old everything, but we should answer their questions simply, honestly, with correct terms and description, and with an attitude that you are happy they are interested. There are appropriate times during the grade school years to introduce birth control and STDs and premarital sex. You can evaluate how much they understand and their level of interest and have age-appropriate conversations that lead to the addition of more meaningful details over time, instead of one, big awkward "Talk" when it's probably already too late. One of my favorite occasions for these more in-depth talks with grade-schoolers is when someone in real life or in a movie gets pregnant in high school. How did it happen? What does it mean? How will her life change? Why might she have done this? What is the boy's role in this situation? What would a better decision be and why?

Remember that goal setting is not magic. Your children may or may not keep their goals. My experience growing up was that it was important that I saw goals as my own. My recommendation is that you let these goals become your kids' goals. It sometimes backfires if you try to make them come to your conclusion. Kids are not dumb, and they will sense if you are pushing them. You are much better off with a kid-chosen goal that is somewhere in the ballpark, but maybe not quite what you want, than a goal that you chose for them, and they perceive it that way.

The beauty of the Follower years is that if you have been involved in their lives and have been transmitting your guidance and values in an atmosphere of respect and love, they will most likely follow your lead and set some very good goals of their own.

Follower Part II – Summing It Up:

So what have we added in this chapter to being present and involved (the most important quality), wiring our kids brains, State Management, school readiness, and describing their world? We have added enrichment and goal setting.

- Enrichment. This is our work to provide contrasting and meaningful experiences for our children. We, as parents, have the best perspective of what experiences would be enriching for our particular kids. Remember that this does not take money, rather our interest and some creativity.
- Goal Setting. This is both finding wants and making plans to get those wants, and helping our kids decide how they are going to deal with all the issues of life. Remember that the Follower years are the best years for these talks. Our children are more likely to adopt our attitudes and values if we have these conversations before sixth grade.

Our kids' tendency to follow because of how their brains develop asks us to be appropriate leaders for them. We must lead them safely into an ever-expanding world and encourage their learning, not only in the academic subjects that school brings, but also the skills such as goal setting that will help them navigate Teen Think in the coming Finder years on their journey to adulthood.

Chapter 7

Filler	Follower	**Finder**	Fulfiller

0..........2.....................11...................18...............25

Finder

This is the chapter many have been waiting for, because the Finder stage brings the unique and well-known challenges of adolescence. To help us understand the Finder stage, let's look at a number of changes that take place in the brain that create significant changes in our kids. I have said the Finder years are approximately from twelve to eighteen years of age.

First, there is an overproduction of potential neural connections in these years, followed by the pruning of the excess connections that are not used. This overproduction is extremely important because it increases our kids' ability to learn the skills they will need to function as adults. These potential neural connections are available in greater numbers so that our kids' learning and experiences can wire their brains to become accomplished in mechanics, nursing, accounting, biology, theatre, basketball, or relationships more easily than we can as adults. At the same time, the brain is then pruning or getting rid of connections that are not being used. As I have mentioned earlier, this excess production of connections seems to clog up the brain, and it does not work as efficiently as it did in the Follower years. One noteworthy side effect of this process, which will be scary to us as parents, is that our teenagers may have a tough time thinking clearly.

Next, certain areas of the brain involved with structures such as the nucleus accumbens come online. These areas will motivate our kids to try new things and gain new experiences. This means they will likely be more ready to take risks and seek novel experiences. Add to this that the areas of the brain that help us exercise good judgment, like the frontal cortex, and the areas that warn us when trying risky things, like the basil ganglia, are not as fully online. This creates another situation that scares parents; our kids seem to want to take risks without having a good sense of what is too risky (especially from the parental perspective).

Add to this that other parts of the brain begin coming online, such as the anterior cingulate gyrus, which can tend to make kids more oppositional. They will become more likely to take the opposite position from us as parents, not because they are intent on deciding against us, but because their brain is causing them to pursue their own perspectives rather than ours. This means they are no longer Followers.

In addition, the emotional areas of the brain begin to come fully online. As with any brain area, as these areas start to function more fully, it takes time for our children to learn how to regulate those functions. Remember what your child went through to learn to control her arms after she was born. First the arms were just jerking around, but over time the movement became much more smooth and controlled. That might be a good way to think about our kids' emotions. For many kids, their emotions definitely jerk around erratically as they come more fully online, and because these systems are complex, it can take a long time for these emotional systems to function predictably.

Finally, on top of all of this, the frontal cortex is not yet fully online. This is the part of the brain that is key in helping us make good decisions. This is also the part of the brain that helps us predict the consequences of actions, control our impulses, be organized, and learn from mistakes.

These changes and other changes I have not listed result in what I call Teen Think. Our teenagers' thinking will tend to be foggy, risky, oppositional, and emotional!

All of the changes of Teen Think are normally combined with the reality that the typical set of conscientious parents has their expectations set by the Follower years. These changes blow their minds! Almost overnight, their child becomes a different kid. He stops thinking clearly, begins taking the opposite opinion, seems motivated to do risky things, has a hard time making good decisions, and unloads emotionally on the nearest person, especially if that person is a parent. Any parent who is not prepared for this can interpret this as defiance and unwillingness of their child to use good judgment. Some will see this as outright rebellion. Often, we as parents can begin to exercise heavy-handed parental authority to try and control our child. This is a bad choice on our part and can create huge amounts of stress. Most of us have been there as parents with stress up to the eyeballs between us and our middle school or high school kids.

It will also help us to understand this potentially volatile situation better by reviewing the effects of stress. What do we know about brains and stress?

Stress can cause brains to function worse than they normally would. During stress, along with adrenaline, chemicals called glucocorticoids are released into the blood stream. These are extremely valuable in promoting behavior that helps us escape danger, such as jumping out of the way of an oncoming car, or running faster than normal to escape a threat.

While these chemicals make the brain alert and skilled at finding a way to escape, they don't help us engage in complex thinking. If stress occurs over long periods of time (say longer than an hour) or is severe, the brain in general doesn't function as well as it should. So if we react negatively or harshly to Teen Think, not only are our kids' brains cloudy, impulsive, oppositional, and emotional, but now we've added to these a general brain function shutdown due to stress. Research is showing that lots of glucocorticoids actually shut down the frontal cortex, the part of the brain that helps us make the hard decisions and think critically about issues. Our negative reaction can actually make Teen Think worse by raising stress levels higher than necessary in our kids. You will recognize this stress response by the deer-in-the-headlights look.

I remember riding through the fog one night at 80 miles an hour in southern Oregon with my dear "Richard Petty-wanna-be" mom. Dad was napping in the back seat, and I was stressed to the max, creating finger indentations on the front dash, as I stared into the fog. Sure enough, two red eyes stared at me through the fog. The deer was frozen by the light. The words, "Mom, there's a deer!" had not fully left my mouth when we crunched that deer.

I've seen kids with the exact same look in their faces. They know they're in trouble. They're stressed. They literally don't know what to do and are frozen in spot, unable to think clearly. The teacher or parent is certain the child should know what to do, and it frustrates them that the kid is just sitting there dumbfounded. The kid sees their parent or teacher becoming more upset, and that only increases the stress and further shuts down their brains. They aren't being obstinate or rebellious; their brains are struggling to function.

One of nature's most basic reactions to potential danger is to immobilize. For many animals, this means they are less likely to be seen by a predator. It should not surprise us that when we get upset with our kids, they may seem to check out.

Why, oh why, does Teen Think happen? Why would our kids be designed to get foggy in their head, become more impulsive, oppositional, and emotional and then have it all get even worse if they're stressed? For my own thinking to understand this, I remember that physically we are animals—very smart animals, but still animals—and we bleed, feed, breed, and develop like animals do.

Think about your average bird for a moment. Why would any young bird in its right mind decide to jump out of a nest 40 feet off the ground when it can't fly? Why would a group of young male monkeys leave their familiar troupe and strike out on a very dangerous course of action to join another troupe? I don't think the birds in the nest have discussions with mom and dad and make a decision to go. Nor do the monkeys have discussions and make these decisions. Rather, changes in their brains motivate them toward these activities.

This may be a stretch for some of us to accept, but like these animals, our kids are not making a conscious decision to change their behavior as much as changes in their brain are motivating them to become their own person, leave the nest, take risks, and get on with becoming an adult. We found that all these changes happened to our kids to one extent or another. The good thing for us is that we had prepared ourselves and our kids for these changes. Therefore, the kids were better able to deal with themselves, we were better able to deal with ourselves, and together all of these changes went pretty well. We can honestly say we loved the teenage years.

What we need to conclude as parents is that our kids are designed to become adults and, in terms of brain development, that process begins in earnest with Teen Think. Our job is to set them free to be adults. Appropriate boundaries need to exist to help them be safe, but safety can very easily be interpreted by parents as a reason to be controlling. That is a huge parental mistake. We can also interpret keeping them safe as keeping them from taking risks. That is also a mistake.

Let's think for a minute where our young teenage children might be in a few short years. They are designed to go out and explore the world and are capable, for example, of incredible accomplishments, as so many young men and women demonstrate in the military. By the age of twenty-two, your son or daughter could be directing missions involving the safety of hundreds of other men and women, utilizing and caring for equipment costing millions of dollars, successfully navigating countless miles through inhospitable and hostile terrain, planning or participating in an intercultural outreach programs to facilitate the rebuilding of a war-torn country's infrastructure, maintaining silence in the face of torture to protect his or her cause, making split-second decisions as to whether a blip on a radar screen is friendly or hostile with thousands of lives at stake, rescuing a fellow soldier in the most dangerous of situations, or boosting the esprit de corps of tired, challenged buddies. Our sons and daughters are capable of so much. We need to set them free to take calculated risks for their own and others' welfare. This begins in earnest around puberty with brain changes designed to make them into men and women.

Note that I say these brain changes take place around puberty. A century ago, however, puberty took place much later, around fifteen to seventeen years of age. Scientists are still trying to figure out why the age of puberty continues to go down. For the purposes of this book, we are going to consider the brain changes of Teen Think to be occurring about the same time in life as the hormonal changes of puberty.

Even with all the great teenage brain understanding I hope to develop in this chapter, the most important information in this book is yet to come. If you have been raising kids and are discouraged that you were not using brain friendly principles and your son or daughter is depressed, defiant, or has simply checked out, the chapter after this should provide hope. In fact, I am convinced that if I failed at every other understanding and recommendation in this book but successfully applied the advice in the next chapter, there will be a good chance that my child will navigate life successfully despite any challenges he or she may face (including my poor parenting).

That's great news, and I sincerely hope I am not overselling the importance of that chapter! One other wonderful aspect of the coming chapter is that it can be applied to one extent or another at any time during the Filler, Follower, Finder, or Fulfiller years. I put it in the Finder years because that is when it is most needed. However, to be prepared for the next chapter, we need to understand the content of this chapter first. So with great hope in mind, let's launch into the bizarre and fascinating world of Teen Think and the teenage brain.

Teen Think Challenges

Let's briefly review and examine what are likely four of the biggest challenges of Teen Think for parenting during the Finder stage. After this brief review, I will point out why these are not so much challenges but opportunities and then deal more in depth with each one.

Challenge #1 – Finders tend to become oppositional. I think that, of all the changes, this is the toughest on parents. If parents have done a good job during the Follower years, kids tend to reflect their parents. Now in the Finder stage, natural brain changes make our children pull away from the Follower stage, and that means to one extent or another pulling away from us. This doesn't feel good, but this change presents the opportunity for them to become their own person with their own values, ideas, and ways of doing things. That is a very good change. Without this change, our kids would be poorly prepared for adulthood.

Challenge #2 – Finders tend to want to try new things and activities, make new friends, and tend to take more risks. This scares us as parents because we see our kids as unaware of the dangers of these risks. Someone could get hurt. The opportunity is that most aspects of life require risk taking. Relationships are risky. Careers are risky. Helping disadvantaged people is risky. Investing for retirement is risky. Having independence is risky.

Learning how to take risks is critical to navigating life successfully. To learn about risks you must begin taking risks. Like decision making, if you learn to take risks earlier in life and deal with the outcomes, the consequences for failure are usually less severe, and the better prepared you are to take risks when the consequences are serious. Taking risks is a good thing. Life would be very dull if we did not enter into commitments and make decisions for which we didn't know the outcome.

Challenge #3 – Finders become seemingly dominated by their emotions at times. This creates drama in the family. The opportunity is that emotions form the basis for good decision making. Slammed doors and stomping feet have a silver lining in our opportunity to help our kids become better decision makers.

Challenge #4 – Finders have a tough time thinking clearly. Their brains are cloudy, their frontal cortex is underdeveloped, and we, as parents, often feel that our kids aren't thinking at all. This is the time of life for our kids to learn new skills because they are developmentally designed to learn them well during this stage.

The opportunity is that the brain is reorganizing itself to function more effectively as an adult and to become able to accomplish adult level tasks.

When these changes begin in your child's brain, childhood is drawing quickly to a close. Nature is producing an adult, and we can't change that. We can either cooperate and encourage that development or resist and fight a losing battle.

Challenge #1 – Opposition

The best situation we could find ourselves in at the beginning of the Finder stage is that we have been preparing for these coming changes for years. As we discussed, the Follower years can be a time of goal setting that develops our children's thinking and decision-making skills, of preparing them for the coming brain and body changes, and of making plans for the adult freedom that should accompany these changes. If that is done, it makes the Finder years easier. For example, as I have said, by the arrival of the Finder years, you should have talked about friends, dating, work, careers, grades, sex, family, drugs, smoking, volunteering, changes in their brains and bodies due to growth, and so on. If you have done this, then when your children tend to become oppositional, they will already have made decisions regarding many of these issues and have a sense of why they feel oppositional. At this stage, our first job as parents is not to freak out when our cooperative little Followers become big oppositional Finders.

When this actually happens to us as parents, we have to resist the urge to panic and instead make ourselves follow a plan to support our kids' transition to adulthood that we, hopefully, have already chosen. Let's imagine we are pro-choice and one day our child comes home and has decided they are going to be pro-life. There are two main ways to respond. We can lobby for our position, or we can try to understand our kids and support their progress to adulthood by encouraging them to think for themselves.

My parents chose lobbying! This is intimidating. Parents are usually larger, more experienced, and can engender a tremendous amount of internal conflict in kids. In my situation, my parents did not understand me, and I did not understand them. They had deeply held convictions, and to have their kids challenge them was traumatic for both parties. I remember wanting to have and hold my own opinions, and I was motivated to fight for my opinions. From a brain development standpoint, we could say that at this time it was more important for me to be forming my *own* opinion than to be forming the *right* opinion. It was impossible to leave the Follower stage, where my opinions were largely someone else's, without adopting my own opinions. To get me out of the Follower stage and into the Finder stage, my brain was motivating me to fight for my own opinions, even if they were lousy opinions.

I had no idea where this motivation was coming from. I had no understanding that parts of my brain were coming online, tending to make me oppositional. The wonderful effect of this change was that I began to think differently and to think for myself. Unfortunately, my parents initially forced me into conflict rather than embracing this change as a necessary step to adulthood.

From a logical standpoint, if parents make this a fight, almost all the ammunition for this conflict is on the parent's side. Parents have already experienced growing through the teenage years, parents have already thought though many issues, and parents have the advantage of years of experience to learn from. From a parental perspective, they have the experience and the right to impose their views. It makes total sense to us as parents to think, *I've already been through this and learned from experience, so why don't you listen to me and adopt my answer?* Unfortunately, imposing our views is exactly the opposite of what healthy brain development needs in the Finder stage. In reality, when we impose our views, we attempt to keep our kids in the Follower stage. If we fight hard enough and actually succeed, we limit our kids' mental ability to think for themselves as adults.

Think of it this way. Often our reaction as parents to the teenage changes is almost like deciding we don't want our toddlers to fall down and skin their knees. The solution we often come to—insisting our teenagers agree with us—is the equivalent of making sure our children don't skin their knees by carrying them everywhere they need to go. We do the walking for them. We know instinctively this is the wrong approach. I don't have to prove it to you with a scientific study. They must walk for themselves and skin their knees, or they will not develop properly. In fact, if we carry them and don't allow them to walk, we will succeed in keeping them from skinning their knees, but they will never learn to walk. That would be an incredible price to pay for protecting them from skinned knees.

This approach would be as ludicrous as feeling my child should believe everything I believe and working diligently to convince him my well-thought-out position is right. By doing this, I essentially do the thinking for him. This does not exercise the part of our kids' brains that needs to be exercised to discover what they are going to believe. Our kids must skin their knees mentally, and we as parents must stand aside and let our kids do it.

Our reaction to these changes is so important. Think of what a disaster it would be to grab your toddler when he falls and say, "I told you that you were not walking correctly! If you don't listen to me, I will have to take away your walking privilege. And don't give me any back-talk, young man. I've shown you how to walk correctly! Now do it!" The measure of our kids' walking success cannot be our walking ability. In the very same way, the measure of our kids' thinking success as developing adults cannot be our thinking ability. For our toddlers, good walking will come, but it will take weeks. We have to be patient and supportive. For our Finders, good thinking will come, but it may take years. We have to be patient and support the developmental process, not impose our ideas and conclusions.

From a brain development standpoint, parents should embrace and encourage this independent thinking as a necessary and appropriate step to adulthood. They should respect the thoughts and conclusions of their kids and encourage them to continue the thinking process. They should not put down, oppose, or belittle their kids' thoughts and conclusions. Rather, they should focus on loving and supporting their kids during this time, while not giving up their parental responsibility. Being responsible as parents means we should give honest and helpful input and feedback on our kids' thinking.

Much of our feedback should be given with a take-it or leave-it attitude. In our own case, we continued to input our views, beliefs, and opinions to our kids, but expected them to learn to use their own heads to make their own decisions. We let them know that, just as we experienced growing up, they would make both good decisions and bad decisions. We resisted our parental urge to scream, "But we already know the answer." At this stage of brain development, the answer isn't the point; rather, developing the thinking process is the point. We were clear with our kids that good decisions make life a whole lot easier and repeated the well-known advice: The only thing wiser than learning from your mistakes is learning from someone else's mistakes.

The exception was the direction and feedback we gave to help our kids stay safe. If we have spent time discussing issues in the Follower years, this will help them keep themselves safe; however, issues will come up in the Finder years in which our kids expose themselves to significant danger. We did not compromise on issues of safety. We, as parents, had to admit our tendency to be overprotective and resist the temptation to make every issue about safety. Parents have to do an honest evaluation of what aspects of their desired feedback has to do with values, opinions, preferences, or beliefs and what aspects are truly related to safety issues.

As parents, my wife and I worked to be as accommodating as we could stomach to our kids' developmental changes and varying opinions and choices. In a real sense, we chose to let ourselves be stressed rather than stressing out our kids in many situations. One of the specific areas where our kids' safety trumped their developmental freedom was driving. Kids get killed in cars because of taking chances and making unwise decisions, and we monitored this area carefully. This was a good example of an area in which our feedback was not optional to accept.

First, we stressed the incredible responsibility and danger of cars through the Follower years into the Finder years. We provided a safe example. We let them know that any violation of the rules of the road would be met with swift and decisive consequences. We also let them know we were legally responsible for them until age eighteen. We insisted on knowing who they were driving with, whether that person was obeying laws such as not having riders in the car until they had been driving for six months, etc., and insisted that they not allow anyone to ride with them until the six months was up (this is an Oregon state law).

I took each one of them driving and provided my training. We sent them all to driving school and then handed them the keys and monitored their progress. The point is that we as parents need to function first as parents, and encourage our children to prepare for adulthood while providing appropriate measures of safety.

I use the phrase *an appropriate measure of safety* because some of us handicap our kids by not providing the opportunity to take enough risks and to learn from those situations. To provide the opportunity for taking risks, our goal was for our kids to have as much freedom by age sixteen in our house as they would have at age eighteen outside of our house. The value of this approach was having two years in which we could provide input and perspective into the kinds of situations that they would face on their own, before they were actually out on their own.

In my own case, Dad eventually engaged me as an adult and let me have my opinions and freedom. This was very helpful for

me and created a sense that he was accepting and validating my
growth into adulthood. My experience was probably typical for a
kid. The more adamant my parents were about their opinion, the
more adamant I was about my opinion. I couldn't always say what I
thought, but I could hold my opposing opinion on the inside. The
more open my parents were, the more open I was. If they let me
hold a position different from theirs, I tended to think about the
options more and was significantly more open to change.

Many parents don't get how this works. They decide to fight
with their kids to make them accept the right way of thinking
from their perspective. This does not allow their kids to think
for themselves and come to their own conclusions. Because their
brain is pushing them to do this, many kids in this situation will
be motivated to simply think the opposite of what their parents
insist on. They are fighting for healthy brain development, and
their parents are unwittingly opposing them. For teenagers in this
situation, the fight becomes a fight for their adulthood. A fight to
decide whether they will get to determine who they are and who
they will become, or whether they will be kept a child for the rest
of their lives.

Some parents are surprised by how adamantly their former
Followers will fight for their freedom. Our perspective as parents
can change if we realize that brain changes are pushing our children
to be self-determining adults. We can take steps to support this
change.

Our goal for the teenage years should be to help set appropriate
safe boundaries, not to take control. There is a vast difference
between the two and a difference in the average reaction of our

kids. From a brain development standpoint, trying to take control will likely push your kids toward rebellion. Planning for age-appropriate boundaries will more likely result in cooperation. This was our experience parenting teenagers.

These responses on the part of our kids can provide a measure for us of how we are doing. In general, are we getting rebellion? We are likely being too controlling. In general, are we getting cooperation? That's a good measure that we are allowing appropriate freedom. Remember, for the most part, brain changes are leading these behavioral changes and responses. It is not that our kids are planning at night how to be uncooperative. This is a good example of the "my brain made me do it" principle. The more we can tune into our kid's responses, the better we can judge whether we are cooperating with these changes.

Let's review what I just said. When we try and control our Finders, their choice of friends, their behavior, etc., we push them toward rebellion or limit their growth as adults. Please let that sink in. I am convinced a significant portion of rebellion in kids is parent motivated. The teenager is asking what can I explore, do, and experience? The controlling parent is pointing out what their kids can't explore, can't do, and can't experience. As parents, we certainly didn't get this right at times, but we did work to focus on what our kids could do, not what they couldn't do.

We loved for our kids to have friends. Whatever kind of friends they could make. We encouraged them to go places with friends, stay over at friends' houses, join clubs with friends, and spend time with friends. In all of this, we continued the discussions from the Follower years and advised on what we thought were appropriate boundaries. We had been clear on the negative consequences of drug abuse, teenage sex, and illegal activity, and continued to be crystal clear. We had begun talking about consequences in the Follower years and continued to make sure they knew they would be the ones living with their choices and to steer clear of dangerous situations. At the same time, we emphasized with our kids that we all make mistakes, and if they made a mistake—even a serious mistake—we would deal with it, make what corrections we could, and move on.

Even our most risk-oriented child responded to this approach. I remember the night that we dropped her off at a party she had wanted to go to. We hadn't driven more than a couple of miles away when we got a phone call. She said that no adult was at the house. This is an issue we had discussed during the Follower years. We talked on the phone, and she came to the conclusion that she would finish saying hello to her friends and then would quietly slip out. At age sixteen, we trusted our kids to be making adult evaluations of situations, and they knew it. Did we expect them to always get the right answer? No, we did not, and we tried to be clear that mistakes provided great opportunities for learning.

We laugh as a family about movies, because the tables turned, and soon we were asking our kids if they approved of a movie for us. They knew our preferences and standards, and more than once we were saved from seeing a lousy movie because our kids would warn us away. Our kids came to understand that we could have different standards, that those standards were subject to change as we learned and grew, and that we would respect and love each other even with differences. They also knew we were deeply committed to their success and safety, and many times we have been rewarded by a phone call or conversation asking our input on what they should do.

In meeting challenge #1, we need to embrace opposition as a necessary step to becoming an adult. As adults, our children must develop in their own way, and they will need the skill of independent thinking. We need to engage oppositional tendencies as healthy in this context and outline their path to adult freedom. We must let them know that this change is coming, and that as they show themselves responsible, we will give them as much freedom as we can.

In summary, how should we communicate this coming oppositional tendency to our kids?

- We need to inform them this shift is coming to one extent or another during the Follower years. We let them know that we will embrace its arrival as an indication of progress toward adulthood, and that this quality will help them become their own person and help them stand on their own.

- We need to be clear that this change will bring differences of opinion. Those differences may cause conflict, but this is okay because it is a healthy developmental step toward adulthood. Learning to engage and resolve conflict is an incredibly important skill to have.

- We need to tell them that part of learning to stand on their own will involve making both good decisions and mistakes. We need to be honest that we made and still make mistakes, and making mistakes is a good way to learn. We will have to deal with the mistakes, but together we will work to look at them as learning opportunities and not as failures.

- In all of this, we will not give up our role as parents. We need to be clear that this means that occasionally we will insist on our position.

It is even possible to harness this oppositional energy to teach our kids to help themselves. Dr. Amen recommends that this oppositional tendency be directed toward negative thoughts within our kids' heads.[12] It is common for teenage kids to have very negative thoughts about themselves or others, and they need to talk back to these thoughts. Do kids with oppositional tendencies know how to talk back? Of course! What should they do when the thoughts come in their heads that they're worthless, ugly, or stupid? Talk back to them! Say internally that they're not worthless or ugly or stupid; they're valuable. They're beautiful and brilliant, each and every one of them, in their own unique way.

By anticipating, embracing, and even harnessing this oppositional energy in our kids, we will help their transition into adulthood by helping them feel loved and accepted, even when these changes put them at odds with us as parents.

Challenge #2 – Taking Risks

Taking risks is closely related to challenge #1. Our kids' oppositional desire tends to heighten at a time when their desire to try new things also heightens. Part of their brain development is pushing them away from the Follower years and the natural safety that those years provided and drawing them to new experiences. Adulthood is filled with new experiences, and getting to practice taking on those new experiences willingly, with enthusiasm, is critical. Here, parental preparation during the Follower years is incredibly important as well.

We talked to our kids about taking risks and presented it as a wonderful thing. Being risky can create feel-good chemicals in our brains. We asked them, however, to take risks for good and not for bad, because both approaches create those same feel-good chemicals. The difference is that taking risks for something worthwhile helps build healthy connections in our brains. Taking risks for bad, while it may feel good at the time, can build habits we will deeply regret later in life. Because of this perspective, we directed our kids early in life into seemingly risky situations for good.

Our daughters volunteered for a service project that would take them to the worst parts of town on Friday nights to bring hope and help to the homeless in our city. This was a risk for good. They didn't do this for the first time on their own; rather, we all had volunteered numerous times as a family in the "dangerous" parts of town during the Follower years. During the Follower years, we had also traveled to Mexico and helped repair homes and central services in a town there.

Our oldest then was not inexperienced when he volunteered to go on his own to Biloxi, Mississippi, to help rebuild homes after Hurricane Katrina. His siblings would follow his example, apart from parental presence. Although they were there with the Red Cross and a group from our church, they were in a potentially dangerous situation, taking risks for good with no parent watching. They would learn that they could tear down destroyed houses and participate in their rebuilding. They would learn that they could contribute to a major project and had skills they didn't even realize.

They would learn that they could make good decisions apart from parents. They saw people in really tough times. They learned that people in tough times can find meaning and hope, and that taking a risk on their behalf was instrumental in bringing that hope.

On another occasion, we stood together as a family in Freetown, Sierra Leone. At that time, Sierra Leone was on the bottom of the world in terms of health and economic development having recently come through a decade-long civil war. We didn't have a well-established organization that we were with, but we went to break ground on how help might be provided. There was risk for all of us, yet taking risks for good is one of our family values, and we have lived according to that value.

Our children got to compare taking risks to help the lives of others, versus some of their friends, who were taking risks that might harm their health or get them pregnant or in other ways affect their lives. Our kids saw the difference firsthand. We wanted them to know that taking risks is important, and that taking risks for good is a great pursuit. In this way, we validated and embraced what their brain development was pushing them toward.

This ability to guide our children's risk taking is another important parental perspective in cooperating with brain development. One option is to protect our children and keep them from risk. Usually we will find ourselves in a battle with our kids, saying no a multitude of times. Because they have no legitimate outlet for risk taking, they smoke, abuse drugs, drive fast, and so on. These activities are often acted out in secret. In a way, these activities can answer a brain development need, the need to learn about taking risks. Unfortunately, they do so in potentially destructive ways.

The opposite approach is actually to provide opportunities for our kids to take risks. As I mentioned earlier, there is the real possibility that our kids may be in situations in which the lives of men and women depend on their abilities by their early twenties. If they are to have the abilities to step up in those situations, we must begin encouraging them toward situations that stretch and challenge them, though they may seem risky.

It is important to remember that this happens on a continuum that may look very different from child to child. Some kids seem designed to take risks, and other kids avoid anything that seems at all risky. In any case brain development happens in a way that we are more likely to take risks in the Finder years than we are in the Follower years. A child who is naturally very conservative may not become a great risk taker, while others will exhibit more extreme tendencies, but all should move toward embracing more risk for healthy brain development.

At this point, it is important to note that even the child who shies away from risks has the same developmental needs. This is an excellent time of life to gain experience in navigating through and handling uncertain situations. They are likely to learn these skills better at this time than during their adult years.

To understand this, I think one good example is when parents don't allow their kids to drive until sometime into their twenties, possibly because the child is conservative and doesn't want to learn, or possibly because the parents are overly cautious. My opinion is, if we wait too long to learn these skills, we will have a tougher time learning them well. Someone who learns to drive at age twenty-seven may end up a lousier driver for life than if they had learned earlier. One fundamental brain-development principle we have discussed is that in general the brain learns new skills more efficiently before the age of twenty-five, and the teenage years are an especially good time to learn skills because of the overproduction of potential neural connections.

Whatever your particular children's tendencies, it is important to open up opportunities for them to stretch themselves. For some kids, an organized activity like playing sports or becoming involved in drama or band may be a stretching experience. For some, stretching themselves may mean they will need to try something on their own, like starting a club or a business. For others, fun social activities like summer camp will provide a stretching experience. The point is that we need to know our kids. Each child will have a different level of comfort with various activities, and the same activity can be routine for one of our kids and an incredible challenge for another.

In our own case, one of our kids found dance to be a stretching experience. We were very happy with her involvement and were surprised when she announced she wanted to quit the dance team. She wanted to leave something she knew how to do well and try drama which was new for her. One of our internal reactions as parents was to lobby for completing the year in dance. However, we valued the skills of risk taking and decision making more than our perception of what would be best.

In this case, we guided the decision-making process. We insisted she talk it through with her coach, list the pros and cons, and told her we would respect and support her decision after she had gone through this process. She followed the process and still concluded she wanted to quit the dance team. She wanted to pursue some other opportunities, and we supported this move. For her, this ended up being an excellent exercise in risk taking and decision making and experiencing what it is like to make a major decision and live with the consequences.

In her case, she did not return to dance during high school, but in her second year of college, she tried out for and succeeded in qualifying for a community dance troupe. This was a fun process to watch and was largely unencumbered by a father- or mother-knows-best approach. Rather, the decision-making muscles in her brain were exercised, and we were rewarded as parents by seeing her take risks, make decisions, and work through them to set her own course in life.

It is important for us as parents to recognize and embrace the fact that our Finders will tend to want to take more risks. We need to see this as a healthy step to adulthood and even look to provide opportunities that allow our kids to stretch themselves by taking risks. This should follow a general developmental pattern from which we are proactive in pursuing some opportunities for them in the later Follower and early Finder years, to where they begin pushing us for opportunities, and we help facilitate as many of those opportunities as we can.

Challenge #3 – Emotions!

In understanding emotional development, information and perspective are key. I remember in my own Finder years, someone shared with me that normal development brings lots of emotional highs and lows during the teenage years. He drew a squiggly line explaining that we would probably feel huge shifts of feelings from high to low, but we shouldn't worry about it. It would all begin to settle out as we went into our twenties and thirties. Believe it or not, I found that information very comforting as a teenager.

Up until that time, I had sensed these huge swings and worried about them. Was I normal? When the world seemed to be ending, was it really ending for me? This five-minute talk stuck in my head, and the next time I was in a bluesy funk, I remember thinking, *If I wait, my mood will probably change.* I waited, and it did. All of a sudden, I had a powerful tool for emotional navigation that consisted of only some very basic information about how our emotions develop.

The tool stuck in my head as simply this: *When I'm feeling crappy about myself, remind myself that emotions naturally nosedive at times, bringing about those crappy feelings. If I wait, my emotions will naturally rebound, and I will feel better.* That little bit of accurate information was incredibly helpful for me not to take my blue times so seriously.

So what information is helpful to us as parents, and what information can we give to our kids regarding emotional development? First, it helps us as parents to know that the emotional changes we see in our kids are very much a result of brain changes that are key to their healthy growth into adulthood. The perspective I personally found most helpful was understanding that emotions are foundational to good decision making.

Remember that the decision-making part of our brain matures late in the growth process. The frontal cortex, which is the most critical area of the brain for making good decisions, is not fully developed until our mid-twenties. Developmentally having the emotional areas of the brain come fully online before the frontal cortex comes fully online is apparently very important for good decision making. This means that in a very real demonstration of how wonderfully our brains are designed, brain development builds the foundation of good decision making in an orderly process. How does this take place?

Eliot, a patient described initially in the book *Descartes' Error* by Antonio Demasio, has given us tremendous insight into the role of emotion in decision making.[13] Eliot underwent surgery for a brain tumor. One of the results of this surgery was Eliot's loss of emotion, or more accurately, the loss of his subjective experience of emotion as feelings.

Eliot can remember that he had emotions, but now is unable to feel emotions. Although his IQ and intellectual capacity are intact and he can very ably state the pros and cons of a choice, he has great difficulty making a decision. Apparently emotion is critical in giving our options a relative measure of importance, thereby aiding us in making decisions. Without emotions, Eliot is apparently unable to act in his own best interest and make good decisions.

One of the possible conclusions of this patient's experience is that our emotional capacity needs to be in place for our decisional ability to work best. Fortunately, in brain development the emotional areas of the brain come more fully online before the primary decision areas. This means that when the frontal cortex is developing, it has a functioning emotional system to work with. This is good. Often we as parents perceive this as bad.

The appropriate way to look at this normal development is that the part of the brain that will eventually help control emotions and help sort them out is not as effective as it could be. So our kids can seem like walking, talking, emotionally dominated, decision-making disasters. This can be a scary perspective for parents, but these feelings of angst result primarily from an incorrect perspective on our part.

If we were having a house built and we expected the house to be warm and keep the rain out as soon as the foundation was laid, we would be in for a rude surprise and a lot of angst. One day, we would get the news the foundation was complete, then head over with our furniture and clothes, and we would find that we got rained on and cold, and that a foundation cannot do the things we expected.

In the same way, we often look at our teenager as if their brains work like ours. It is incredibly unnerving if you expect your teenager to be able to assess their emotional state and use that assessment and their emotions in conjunction with logical thinking to make great decisions. For most teenagers, that is not going to happen. The foundations of decision-making ability are being built. Since one of those foundations is emotional capacity, many Finders will behave as if they are dominated by emotions. As they continue to develop and exercise their frontal cortex, that emotional dominance will lessen.

This leaves us in the position of having a person in our house, for whom we are legally responsible, who can be emotionally all over the map and driven by those emotions. This is scary unless you know that this state is the necessary and appropriate step to good decision making just as a foundation is a necessary and appropriate step to a house that is warm and keeps out the rain.

We can help our kids in two ways. The first way is our attitude. When those feet stomp down the hall and the door slams or our child stews in a sulky silence for the first time, instead of freaking out, we can say, "This is okay! The road to good decision making has begun in earnest," and welcome this change as a necessary process that will benefit our kids greatly as adults.

We can also understand that our parental job changes at this point. We are not to take their emotions as a subject to deal with directly and correct as if they were right or wrong. Rather, we need to embrace and accept them for what they are—a work in progress. They are developing and far from perfect, just like a toddler learning to walk. As they develop, these emotions will help our kids have opinions about school, teachers, us as parents, driving, and friends, and these emotions will push them to make decisions. Those decisions will likely be lousy as with any process we are new at. We can then root for our kids as we see the emotional foundation of their decision-making capability develop.

The second way is the information we give our kids. I keep pushing this, but we should have let them know during their Follower years that soon their emotional capability will be coming more fully online, and that will be a great and crucial step to their becoming a successful adult. One of the best opportunities to have this conversation is when they, as a Follower, see an older cousin, friend, or sibling have an emotional event. Ask them what they think about it. Most sensible Followers will say it was ridiculous. This opens the door to explain this developmental process. As hard as it may be for them to believe, they will go through this, and these changes will provide a great opportunity for them to become good decision makers.

Let's look at one example that happened in our home. My wife and I were sitting as a family at the dinner table when our middle-schooler announced that her math teacher was "such a jerk." To set the stage for how my wife and I handled this statement, let's review a couple of things. First, we've taught our kids to respect others, and they knew calling someone a jerk was not the way to show respect. Second, this child would have never done this in the Follower stage. So either our child was willfully tossing out her manners and disrespecting our upbringing, or something else was going on.

My parents would have thought I was disrespecting their standards and being rebellious. Their immediate response would have been shock that I would speak of a teacher that way, and they would have corrected me and delivered a speech about respecting my elders. That would have been the end of the talk, and unfortunately, the end of any hope of any of us learning through discussion.

If they had been a bit more thoughtful, they might have reasoned something like this. *Rick does not normally disrespect a teacher like this, so he knows how to respect them, maybe something else is going on. Let's engage him in conversation and see where this goes.*

Because my wife and I had a clue about emotional development, we bit our tongues and resisted giving speeches in this particular instance. Instead of reacting, we engaged the conversation and steered it in a learning direction. "Really, what happened?" we asked. Our daughter began to describe some behavior on her teacher's part that she found very annoying. We listened, talked, and basically agreed that from time to time throughout our lives we will run into annoying teachers and bosses. What we recommended to our daughter as the next step was that we figure out what was causing the annoyance and the best way to deal with it.

We recognized that her emotional capacity was coming online. This meant that it would not be very accurate at times. At times it would be blown out of proportion. This was a new ability; how could we expect it to be well-developed and accurate? At this point, it was important not to criticize her developing ability. As I've said before, this would be something like yelling at her as a toddler, because she doesn't walk very well. What did we do with our toddler when she made horrifically failing attempts at walking? We praised her and got all gushy over it, because she was trying. What do we usually do with our middle-schoolers when they make horrifically failing attempts at emotional responses? We criticize. That is not right. We need to affirm and encourage their entrance into the world of emotions just as we affirmed and encouraged their entrance into the world of walking...bumps, bruises, and all.

This is difficult because we will feel personally attacked as parents. Their immature attempts at emotional responses will be spread to everyone around them, including us. We are often tempted to react when we feel we are being criticized. While we should teach our children how to express their feelings with respect, this is secondary to affirming their emotional learning at this point in their development.

How did our daughter benefit when we engaged her critical remarks for her teacher rather than correct her? First, she began to find expression for what she was feeling inside. This expression helped her identify her emotions and provided practice in expressing and engaging those emotions. Second, she also learned more about what she did and did not like and how she would deal with situations in the future that were unacceptable to her. These were important lessons.

This is critical because I have met too many people who mistrust their internal senses and are taken advantage of by people in positions of authority. Wrong and inappropriate behavior is wrong and inappropriate even if a very important person does it. I wanted my kids to learn what their internal senses mean, and how to use those senses to their benefit.

What did our daughter learn in this case? She learned that this teacher was very disorganized and, as a result, wasted her time. My daughter hates situations that waste her time. Engaging her response helped us have a very important continuing conversation over the coming years. From this experience, our daughter has been helped to trust her senses and has avoided numerous situations in which her time would have been wasted. Because she could not change teachers, we also worked on what she should do if she is stuck in a similar situation. All of this was learned because we let her say her teacher was a jerk and engaged that statement as a part of her emotional learning. Note that as parents we did not agree with her that her teacher was a jerk; rather, we took the opportunity to validate her emotions and encourage her emotional development and understanding.

One more comment about emotions. Keeping in mind that emotional development helps form the basis for good decision making, many of us have had the common experience that boys in general (not always) have a more difficult time figuring out what they want to be when they become adults or are very good at saying, "I don't know," when asked their opinion. That makes sense when you consider the role of emotions. Boys are generally behind girls in their emotional development. So it would follow that, on average, girls are better or faster decision makers at an earlier age.

This is yet another good reason not to squash emotional responses. What is needed is not the suppression of emotions, but their expression and engagement. By taking this approach, we will help our children become better decision makers.

Challenge #4 – Foggy Thinking

At times your Finder's head will seem like it is in a fog. Maybe it will seem like that all the time during their teenage years. The explosion of neural connections that creates this fog is necessary for them to become adults, but it produces what can appear to be a step backwards in their ability to think.

As I have already said, although a Follower's brain is in the process of developing as well, it *seems* more efficient and effective than a Finder's brain. The primary objective of a Follower's brain is learning from examples and reproducing their attitudes and behaviors. These are much simpler tasks than a child growing into adulthood, taking charge of his or her life, and figuring out what that involves. This is what a Finder's brain must do.

So while both the Follower and the Finder brains are uniquely suited to their particular tasks, a Follower's brain seems to work better to the casual observer. A Follower would not be well-suited to become an independent adult or to be a mom or dad responsible for a family. Followers are rather well-suited to be a part of the family and learn from us as parents. This is naturally more comfortable for parents than the Finder stage. In the Finder stage, our kids are well-suited to becoming an independent adult over time. That means pulling away from us and figuring things out for themselves. You should already be concluding what this means for us as parents. We need to have an appropriate understanding and attitude toward this and need to prepare our kids for this process.

First let's evaluate our attitude. What good is happening during this foggy brain time for our kids? Our kids' brains are creating tons of new neural connections and getting rid of unused connections. This allows them to learn new tasks and skills with relative ease and speed. For example, the early Finder years may provide the last window of opportunity to learn a language in such a way that one sounds like a native speaker. If your child decides they really like drumming, their brain is making a bunch of connections available that can be used to learn drumming. If they practice drumming, the brain will more quickly establish the connections required for them to become a proficient drummer. They can learn drumming (or any other skill) later in life, but as most of us have experienced, this is usually a more difficult process.

Our attitude should be one of gratefulness and anticipation for the fog, because it signals that the ability to take on adult responsibility is beginning. If nothing else, this fog is largely what will help them become capable to move out of the house one day and support themselves. That ought to be a cause for us as parents to celebrate the fog!

We should also inform our Follower that the fog is coming and let them know its purpose. Our kids will be familiar with growth spurts and that sometimes growing pains, clumsiness, or things like acne can accompany these changes. This fog is a kind of growth spurt for the brain. Just as kids experience growth spurts differently and some kids have more joint pain, clumsiness, or acne than others, so this growth spurt in the brain will not be the same for everyone. Most Finders will experience a time in which their brain doesn't seem to work quite as well. They might have a tough time remembering things that used to be easy to remember. They might stop noticing fairly obvious things, and this new characteristic might surprise and frustrate us as parents that they can be so oblivious. Sometimes when teachers and parents explain things to Finders, the explanations will not make sense to them.

We should prepare our Finders that sometimes teachers and parents can act frustrated when they seem slow to understand. This is unfortunate, but most adults aren't familiar with brain development and don't understand this change. It is very reasonable to encourage our Finders to tell an adult that they wish to understand, but they need the adult to repeat what was said, or explain it, or give them time to think about it. One young adult I know was incredibly encouraged when his math teacher showed an understanding of how brains work.

Part of the way into the year, over two-thirds of this young man's high school freshman math class was failing, and he as a student was feeling stupid and a failure. He related that his whole high school experience changed when the teacher admitted that, as a teacher, he was responsible for their learning, and if that many kids were failing, something was wrong with his teaching, not with the students. The teacher changed how he was teaching, and in fairly short order, the percentages reversed and two-thirds of the class was passing. This change helped this particular student learn math, but more importantly, as he related, this experience taught him he wasn't stupid.

This is a huge lesson for understanding kids in the Finder stage. They can learn and can learn exceptionally well; it just takes time for the brain to sort out all the neural connection possibilities that are provided during this time of life. The more we can have patience and provide encouragement, the more our Finders will cooperate with us.

Why, Why?

One question that our Finders will become more adept at using and is a characteristic of Teen Think is the simple question "Why?" In fact, some teenagers will become so good at using this question that we as parents will suspect it is part of a carefully contrived scheme to have us institutionally committed for insanity so they can go live with someone else. This is, in fact, not true at all. As I have said, the teenage ability to drive parents crazy is not contrived; it simply comes naturally to them.

Thinking of what we have learned about the brain and stages of development, the habit of asking *why* should make good sense. If brain development is pushing kids to become independent, take risks, make decisions, and make new connections by learning new things, they need to understand why as much as possible. The why of something is incredibly important; it helps us have the right understanding, it helps us reason, and therefore it helps us make the right decision.

This questioning is one of those items that comes in the "my brain made me do it" category. Why? Why? Why? The brain is thirsty for meaning, for how to think about issues, and how to have good information to make decisions, so *why* is an excellent question for this kind of brain to ask. There is often a problem however.

The problem becomes apparent when your compliant Follower appears to become reticent (the fog), begins to pull away from you and takes questionable risks (nucleus accumbens coming online), opposes you (cingulate gyrus coming online) when he or she used to be so sweet and cooperative, and on top of that questions everything.

You can think all sorts of inappropriate parental thoughts like, *The kid is rebelling and questioning my authority as a parent! He doesn't appreciate all I've done! She doesn't trust me! What did I do to deserve this? Why, oh why, do I have to explain everything? Then when I explain and give a good reason, the kid argues! I mean, this is outright disrespect. Who does this kid all of a sudden think he is?*

This is wrong, wrong, wrong thinking on our part.

The brain is trying to learn and figure things out and asking why is a simple, effective, easy-to-remember way of helping the brain do this. The Follower stage in which you said, "Because I said so," and they said, "Okay," is gone. In fact, during the mid- to late-Follower years, we should develop the habit of explaining and resist using the phrase "because I said so." This will help us have the habit of giving explanations in place by the Finder years.

Again, the difference will be when we explained why in the Follower years, likely the child said okay. When we explain why in the Finder years, we will likely hear "Why?" again.

We are still the parents, and we need to be clear with our kids that during the Finder years, we will have to deal with times when we disagree. During those times of disagreement, we reserve the "because I said so" right. We will try to use this right sparingly. However, because we love our kids, are working for their welfare, and are still legally responsible, every once in a while, even though they don't understand, we will exercise the parental prerogative and simply say something has to be a certain way. Don't expect this to be met with warmth and praise. Likely we will at least get the cold shoulder. No matter what reaction we get, we need to hang tough, be the parents, and insist on whatever we consider to be nonnegotiable for our kid's safety.

Our attitude needs to be one in which we don't criticize our kids for poor or inadequate thinking or decisions. Rather, we support them and praise them for working through issues. To emphasize, I will use the example again of our kids learning to walk. They don't need our criticism and pointing out their errors in the toddler stage; they need our appreciation and excitement that they are trying, even though it often involves failing, in their learning to walk.

Kids need the same support when thinking through issues, trying to understand, and using their often inadequate understanding to make decisions. First, we need to resist the tendency to focus on whether their decision is optimal or not. Be happy they're trying.

Second, just like we held our toddler's arms and helped them learn to walk, our kids need our guidance. We need to point out that they are making good progress in the skill of decision making, and then offer our opinions for them to accept or reject and support them in their decisions.

Finders and Decision Making

What are some important steps in good decision making? Helping our kids express what they want is a good place to start. Then we should ask them to imagine how their life would be if they get what they want. We should also help them figure out optional ways to get what they want and which might be better, and then support them in their decision.

To begin with, we should ask our children what they want and how they think their life will be if they get it or do it: for example, to become an Eagle Scout by age seventeen, or to decide between going to camp or going to Grandma and Grandpa's (G&G) place in Lake Tahoe for a week during the summer. Let's say your daughter, now a middle-schooler, has been going to G&G's for a week every summer, but because G&G are traveling this summer, there is only one week available. This is the same week as camp.

A couple of interesting things can happen here. It could be that G&G are somewhat possessive of seeing their grandkids, and they only get to see their princess one week a year and play on our emotions by stating, "Is it too much to ask to see our grandchild one week of the year?" Parents can mess with their kids' heads at this point. You can repeat G&G's line and put pressure on your daughter to go see G&G. This would amount to teaching your daughter what G&G want. You could view this from your own perspective, insisting she should go, knowing secretly that your lives will be easier for the next six months, not having to listen to G&G criticizing and complaining. This would be teaching your daughter what you want as parents. A Finder does not primarily need to know what G&G want or what her parents want; a Finder needs to discover what she wants.

This is an example of the real learning that is needed for healthy brain development during the Finder years; helping your child figure out what he or she wants. The Filler and Follower years are great years to be introducing values, such as considering the needs of others and knowing how to put others first. If you live these values and teach your children these values, your Followers will learn them and do them (and they will seem like such angels at times).

However, these are not the primary needs of the Finder. The Finder needs to understand what they want, and then as they mature, they can decide (knowing full well what they want) to give that want up at times to benefit another person. I've seen too many Finders still being pushed by parents to do what everyone else wants them to do. This is very confusing for kids and does not help them find out who they are.

So you ask your daughter, "What do you really want to do?" "I don't know," is a common response. This is a golden opportunity. Depending on the child, she could be saying, "I like going to G&G's, and it is fun and all, but I really want to go to camp with my friends, but can I say that? Won't G&G be hurt?" The opportunity is to point out how important it is for her to know what she wants. As an adult she will make decisions that will impact her life, and she will live with those decisions. Training her to allow someone else to make her decisions; whether it's G&G (don't go to camp), or parents (go to G&G's), or a boyfriend (let's have sex); is not healthy because primarily she, not they, will live with the consequences of those decisions.

Let's assume she says she doesn't know what she wants. As parents, we need to be patient with these responses. This is a great chance to work on information gathering and envisioning. Information gathering has to do with figuring out what we know and what we can find out to help us make the decision. In this case, we can think about what happened the previous summer. "Yes, G&G were great, and I had fun, but at camp I made some really great friendships that I enjoyed all year long." Then envision what would happen this summer. "I'd have fun at G&G's, but I think I would miss being with my friends more."

Once you have a good possible decision, think whether there are any alternatives. Could she visit G&G on a long weekend this year at another time? Don't angle for her to make the decision you might make. Simply help her understand her preferences and the possibilities.

Then encourage her to make the decision that she thinks best. Be supportive of her decision and help run interference for her with G&G if necessary. You can give her words to say, "G&G, I enjoy seeing you guys so much, but I've decided to go to camp that week this summer." If G&G start applying pressure, you may need to step in. The playing field is not level between most kids and adults, and G&G can exert a lot of pressure. Let G&G know you have a young adult who very much needs to learn to make her own decisions, and you support her in this.

Then plan to review. After the week of camp, check in, "What do you think of your decision?" "Did it go as you expected?" Here again, a couple of things could happen. It could have been a great week. In this case, her decision-making ability will be reinforced. She could have broken her ankle and ended up in the hospital. If this happened, it is very important to give positive feedback, and let her know that even when we make good decisions, we can't control everything. The unexpected happens, and you can help her understand how she learned some valuable lessons in dealing with the unexpected.

If something went wrong, G&G may come through with an "I told you so" attitude. This should also be discussed. Let her know that we may get criticism for our decisions, but that often has nothing to do with whether it was a good decision or not.

It could be that she will conclude her decision was not a good one. If that is the case, let her know you've made plenty of bad decisions as well. Let her know that usually something beneficial can come out of these situations, even if it is simply knowing how to avoid a similar situation in the future. The main point is that as a Finder she needs to learn to own her decisions, their benefits, and their consequences. That is the only way she will become a better decision maker.

We as parents must learn to embrace and support the process of learning to be a decision maker. It will take years. Many times our kids will not know what they want, and this can be related to normal brain development as well. If our kids' emotions come online more slowly or are more subdued, they may be naturally more ambivalent about things. We need to be patient and supportive.

Sometimes our kids will seem controlled by emotions and will make and reverse decisions. This is not the time to criticize or make fun of them, but to encourage (*I'm glad to see you're working through all the pros and cons*), and to remind them of what we've (hopefully) taught them about good decision making during the Follower years.

During this time of life, it really helps us as adults to have someone to commiserate with; someone with whom we can share our frustrations. This will help us give supportive responses to our often frustrating kids. As adults and parents, we need to be thoughtful and supportive in our responses no matter how much we would like to blow up. But whatever our internal response is to the latest Finder crisis, we need to control our responses for their benefit. I should pause and say that I am using G&G as an example, but I am not speaking from personal experience in our family. Our grandparents and so many grandparents are very helpful in allowing kids to make decisions and grow up.

The Olden Days and Decision Making

I am not an "olden days" type of person. I think every generation has its strengths, weaknesses, and challenges. So I have never wished to return to any olden days; however, we can learn from what has happened before.

In the area of decision making, I think we've lost some natural training in recent years. One of the changes many of us as parents have made is becoming very active in scheduling our kids' time. From the early years, we decide for our kids what activities they are involved in, and how those activities will be scheduled. We see this as helping them get ahead in sports and education. There are some advantages to this, but I think there are also disadvantages, and the greatest disadvantage in my opinion comes in the area of decision making.

When I was a kid, whether for good or bad, I largely determined what my schedule was outside of school. I played football, basketball, and baseball, rode my neighbor's motorcycle in the field behind our house, caught tadpoles and tried to grow frogs, built forts in the woods, biked all over our town, worked picking berries in the summers to afford skiing in the winters, mowed lawns for money and repaired and tuned up lawnmowers, snuck into the woods to try cigarettes, failed miserably at making money by babysitting, failed miserably at shoplifting, hiked with friends to the top of the nearest mountain, and decided I didn't like the taste of whisky, all before I was thirteen and mostly without parental direction.

From early grade school on, I was making all kinds of decisions about how to spend my time, what to do, and how to get myself out of sticky situations. It was the "olden days." In the summer, Mom would give me breakfast, and out the door I would go, show up for lunch, show up for dinner, and be racing in the house just before the street lights came on at night (if you hit the door after those lights came on, Dad's belt hit your rear). There were things I was expected to do such as chores around the house, church on Sunday, charitable activities such as visiting people in convalescent homes, and going places with my parents—but aside from those things and school, my schedule was largely my decision.

Is this a perfect scenario? No way! But it was great exercise for the decision-making part of my brain. I had made tons of decisions and experienced lots of successes and failures by the time I hit the Finder years. Even though the decision area of my brain had not yet fully myelinated, it had plenty of exercise, and lots of connections had been created. I don't remember struggling much over major decisions later in life, such as what courses to take in high school, or what college to attend.

Did I make the best decisions? No. In fact, it would have been helpful to have more input from my parents. Sometimes I remember being frustrated by their lack of input. I think there were key times I could have made better decisions with their help, especially about things I had no experience, such as college. But as it was, there was no lack of decision-making experience in my growing up, and I did not hesitate to make decisions.

It is my opinion that we make too many decisions for kids. It is not unusual for kids to get into high school having made very few decisions of any real importance. It becomes a problem when they, as high-schoolers, try to decide where to go to college. All of a sudden, they are making life-changing decisions with little experience.

One way I like to look at this is to make a graph of the situation. On the bottom of the graph, I put age. Up the left-hand side, I put the importance or consequence of decisions. The younger we are, the less importance or consequence our decisions usually have. As we grow older, especially into the Finder years, decisions can have long-lasting consequences. We are dealing with decisions that will affect our college life, work choices, and sometimes our marriage.

Decision Importance/Consequence

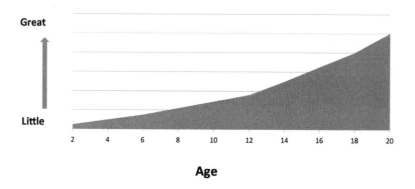

When would we like to get a lot of practice at decision making? Do we want to be new at this in high school? I don't think so. I would want my kids to make as many decisions as they can, as early as they can, to get good decision-making experience. The earlier they make and learn from lousy decisions, the less importance and negative consequences those decisions have. I don't think I can overemphasize this. If we make the right decisions for our kids, their decision-making abilities don't get exercised, and they don't become good decision makers. The brain learns far more from making errors and correcting those errors than it does from someone providing the right decision or answer.

I am not advocating turning your kids free like I was when I was a kid. We don't live in the same society. However, I am advocating for allowing kids to make as many of their own decisions as they can as early as they can. We need to guide the process and keep them safe.

By including an active goal in our child raising of letting them make numerous decisions early in life and requiring them to work out the results of those decisions with our input, we prepare them to be better decision makers during the Finder years.

Finder – Summing It Up:

In this chapter we have looked at some of the characteristics of Teen Think and how to deal with them. The most important aspect of dealing with them is our understanding and attitude toward them. Those characteristics were opposition, risk taking, the domination of emotions, and foggy thinking.

- Opposition is good because it is necessary for our children to become adults. It means brain changes are forcing them to think in new ways that distinguish them from their parents. If we work together with our Finders, this oppositional tendency is healthy for their growth into adulthood.
- Risk taking is good because our kids need practice at taking risks. Life is full of necessary risks. Directing them into risk taking for good is incredibly helpful for our Finders.
- Emotions are good because they lay the foundation for good decision making. As with any new developmental system, our kids emotions will be erratic and unreliable. That's okay! By

supporting their emotional growth, we will be rewarded with better decision makers.

- Foggy thinking is good because it gives our kids the capacity to learn adult skills and aptitudes. Our task as parents is to be patient during this time and support our kids while their brains sort out all of the learning necessary for them to succeed as adults.

We then finished the chapter talking about decision making. We will see in the next chapter that figuring out who we are and what we can contribute are probably the most important factors in navigating the Finder and Fulfiller years successfully.

Chapter 8

Filler	Follower	**Finder**	Fulfiller

0..........2....................11...................18..............25

A Vision for the Finder Years

T his is it! This may be the most important chapter of this book. If you understand and do what is recommended here and nothing else, there's a decent chance your kids will do okay in the long run. While only doing what is recommended in this chapter is not ideal, as our kids may have to navigate unnecessarily difficult times, understanding and applying this chapter's advice can make up for a lot of mistakes. Kids have a tremendous ability to navigate even the most difficult times when they're motivated.

When I think of this subject, I can't help but think of Dr. Seuss. Remember his book, *Oh, the Places You'll Go!* and how it starts.[14]

Congratulations!

Today is your day.

You're off to Great Places!

You're off and away!

You have brains in your head.
You have feet in your shoes
You can steer yourself
any direction you choose...
OH! THE PLACES YOU'LL GO!

There are so many places to go, and there is so much to do. The problem is that many kids are unmotivated and too discouraged to try. What will motivate our kids to take this journey toward adulthood in a productive way? The solution lies in giving our kids an understanding of who they are and a vision for what they can do.

I think we've all had the experience of meeting someone who, despite huge challenges growing up, has done a great job of building a successful life with purposeful work and good relationships. What happened in this person's life? Why did he or she do so well when so many others gave up in the same difficult circumstances or gave up in even better circumstances? Why do some kids with great advantages seem to spin their wheels and waste their time getting into trouble? Why do others, without those advantages, surmount challenges and succeed?

The path to this kind of resilient spirit has to do with our kids understanding their strengths and gaining a vision for what they can accomplish. The good news is that if we help our kids with this, they will likely do well. There is hope then, no matter how fantastic or not-so-fantastic we've been at parenting. Even though we may regret what we have or haven't done, there is reason to believe that our kids can be motivated to work through issues and go great places and do great things. Isn't that fantastic news?

I'm going to approach this subject in a way that we can begin working on it at almost any time—Filler, Follower, Finder or Fulfiller. I have put this in the Finder section since it is related to our children finding out who they are, and this stage is the most critical time for our kids to gain this understanding and vision. The reality is that it is never too late to start working on this.

There are at least three areas we can work on. First, it will help if we give our kids a sense of their temperament. Second, it is critical to help our kids gain a healthy perspective of their traits and take advantage of them. I am going to define *traits* as "strengths and weaknesses." Finally, and most important, it is critical for our kids to gain a vision for what they can do.

Let's begin with *temperaments*, or what we might call "natural personality styles." We used a very simple system to teach our kids about temperament. My wife and I had watched a video series before we had kids called *Homes of Honor*.[15] There was a bunch of great information in this series and a simple way to remember temperament types. I had been taught in psychology classes about the four basic temperaments, but I could never remember the names. I think one was phlegmatic, and I cannot tell you what it means to this day.

However, this series taught me about personality types through lions, otters, beavers, and golden retrievers. I was familiar with all these animals and could build a bridge of understanding between these animals and personality types. A lion is a leader, an otter is around to have fun, a beaver pays attention to detail, and a golden retriever is as faithful a friend as you could want. I could picture this in my head. Obviously, this is not all there is to learn about personality types, but it provides a good place to start.

Our oldest was a lion. At two years old, if you didn't have a plan for the day first thing in the morning, he did. It amazed us how strong this personality type was at such an early age. We hadn't sent him to leadership school, or had him listen to inspirational tapes, yet he was leading our family "pride" almost from day one. Fortunately, my wife was a lion as well and quickly learned to arrive at the crib with a plan.

Our second was an even combination between a golden retriever and a beaver. Again, we were amazed by her distinct personality. Very early on, she knew there was a right way to do things and she insisted things be done her way (the right way—beaver). There were definitely the right kinds of clothes to wear. If we chose the wrong clothes, she would let us know. Although she had distinct preferences, she didn't want to be confrontational about getting her way, and was as responsible and faithful a friend as a kid could be (golden retriever).

Our last was a party waiting to happen (otter). She has a bit of golden retriever in her as well and avoids conflict. So the word "no" is not naturally in her vocabulary and "why not?" is her trademark phrase, especially if there is fun involved.

The great thing was that Gary Smalley and John Trent (who produced *Homes of Honor*) also co-authored a children's book along with Cindy Trent and Norma Smalley called *The Treasure Tree*, which is a children's story about personality types based on these different animals. So from early on in our house, the kids learned about their natural personality bent through our reading this book as a family.

We would tell our oldest, "You're a lion and that's really good, because you have talent to direct and lead people and projects. You can do great things with that talent." Our second learned early on that she could make good decisions and had clear ideas about what was fair and right. She could help other people make good decisions and had a great talent for being a faithful friend. Our third learned early on that she could get along with almost anyone and bring enjoyment into situations and people's lives. Her personality caused her to be calm, relaxed, and collected even in dangerous situations, making her great with animals and clear-headed in pressure situations.

We also told them that each of us could easily get out of balance because of our personalities. If a lion always has to be in charge, this would likely cause conflict, tire the leader out, and others would not get chances to lead. So taking turns and learning to follow were important lessons for our lion.

It is good for a beaver to have a clear idea of what is right, but sometimes the world is complex and other people have different ideas. So we had to introduce the idea of grey areas to our daughter. Sometimes people can't see it her way, and she had to learn to work together anyway.

Golden retrievers can be faithful to a fault. Helping people is a very admirable quality, but sometimes retrievers can enable other people's problems, because they don't want to confront issues. Setting proper boundaries to protect themselves, such as saying no or facing a problem head-on, is very important.

Otters love to have fun, and this makes them popular with people. Life can't always be fun and games, however, and some otters end up with very messed-up lives, because they never learned to be responsible, set priorities, and take care of the necessary tasks in life.

We taught our children that they had wonderful natural personality qualities, and that those qualities still needed to be developed and monitored to serve themselves and others well. Because we had the children's book, this learning began in the Filler stage in our household and continues to be a subject of discussion to this day. Even though we can change over time, it is still good to recognize our natural personality tendencies, work with them, and make use of them in our life choices.

Do you need to use the lion, otter, beaver, golden retriever methodology? Absolutely not. It worked well for us. Use it only if it makes sense to you. The point is to work to identify your kids' personalities, help them understand their personality tendencies, and then talk about their personalities in a way that shows them the incredible value of who they are. This is tempered by explaining that any strength carried to an extreme can become a weakness, so we not only have to learn to value our personality qualities, but also learn how to appropriately use them and how to know if we are out of balance. This is great information for our kids to have in the Finder years as they try to find out who they are.

Since I may have piqued your interest in this particular system, and we found it to be kid friendly, here is a list of the animals and the qualities they show, taken from the *Homes of Honor Manual*.[16]

Lion—Takes charge, determined, assertive, firm, enterprising, competitive, enjoys challenges, bold, purposeful, decision maker, leader, goal driven, self-reliant, adventurous.

Phrase—Let's do it now!

Beaver—Deliberate, controlled, reserved, predictable, practical, orderly, factual, discerning, detailed, analytical, inquisitive, precise, persistent, scheduled.

Phrase—How was it done in the past?

Golden Retriever—Loyal, non-demanding, even keel, avoids conflict, dislikes change, adaptable, sympathetic, thoughtful, nurturing, patient, tolerant, good listener.

Phrase—Let's keep things the way they are.

Otter—Takes risks, visionary, motivator, energetic, very verbal, promoter, avoids detail, fun-loving, likes variety, enjoys change, creative, group oriented, mixes easily, optimistic.

Phrase—Trust me! It'll work out!

Next, I think it is important to help our kids understand their traits in terms of strengths and weaknesses. What do I mean by this? Well, one distinct example of a trait would be if a child has Attention Deficit Hyperactivity Disorder (ADHD). I have had some great mentors in understanding this trait. I originally thought of ADHD as only a problem; hence the label "disorder." There are certainly aspects of ADHD that are a problem, but that is not the whole story. I remember hearing Dr. Hallowell give a talk in which he described the ADHD brain as a Ferrari brain with Model T brakes.[17] In other words, a kid with ADHD has a really great brain; he just needs to work on the parts that help him slow down and pay attention.

What did he mean by this? What's great about ADHD? Having ADHD himself, Hallowell explained that a lot of people with ADHD are very creative. They don't see the world in the same way as other people. Creativity usually comes from a unique perspective. People with ADHD can be wonderfully spontaneous and have great curiosity. If they are hyperactive, it is likely that they will have a lot of energy in life. If you put creativity and spontaneity together with a lot of energy, you can become incredibly successful. Many people with ADHD have.

Is there a problem with ADHD? Absolutely. Researchers can tell you the prisons are full of people with ADHD. If ADHD is not addressed, kids can become extremely frustrated with the expectations and requirements of our social systems (like school) and give up. As we all know, school normally requires that students sit still, focus, listen, respond, and complete homework. All of this can be very challenging to someone with ADHD.

My task in this chapter is not to solve ADHD. I am not qualified. However, I can comment on how parents, teachers, and other influential people look at a trait like ADHD. I have been convinced that the world of medicine has already presented our kids with a challenge by naming this a disorder. As I have pointed out above, it is not necessarily all bad. However, if I were a kid and had been slapped with a "disorder" label, that could be discouraging if not handled correctly. Labels can be really nasty things, and sometimes more of a disadvantage than the condition the child faces.

I don't think it is a stretch for anyone to imagine that if I were labeled with a disorder, other people would be tempted to interpret my life in light of my disorder, which could make me focus on my disorder and cause me to feel limited by my disorder. Kids can literally become depressed in grade school, because they feel like they will be failures or stupid their entire lives. Someone sometime has to show them their strengths and give them hope.

I think it is helpful for parents to list their kids' strengths and weaknesses. Our child may get a label from a counselor or a teacher. We shouldn't despair; rather we should work to find out everything that is good about that particular trait as well as the disadvantages. Understanding both the strengths and weaknesses allows us to play a key role in helping our child. Along with working on the weaknesses, we need to tell our child their strengths (because the professionals may not) and then support them in improving their weaknesses and capitalizing on their strengths. Kids also need to know that everyone, whether they have a label or not, has strengths and weakness, just like they do.

As an example, let's say a child is very uncoordinated. There are a couple of ways we can approach this. Some of us might pressure the child to perform physically beyond his or her abilities and react with disappointment when they don't do well. That is tough on a kid. It is far more important to encourage that child. That encouragement might happen because we seek to understand his or her strengths, and our primary focus is on those strengths; rather than the fact that he or she is uncoordinated. We might have this encouraging perspective because we are uncoordinated ourselves, we have learned to accept this trait with humor, and have found how to be successful in other ways. It could be that when we notice this clumsiness, we focus on large motor skill development and work with the child, throwing in lots of encouragement and support until he or she is not so clumsy. However we do this, it is critical to recognize our kids' strengths and praise them for what they can do, the progress they do make, and to dearly love them even if their heart is not into football, basketball, or some other sport like ours is.

Are there any advantages to being uncoordinated? We may get to spend more time on activities outside of sports. These days, sports take an inordinate amount of time, and not having to keep the sometimes insane schedules that go along with sports is helpful. As I mentioned above, if children's parents and teachers help them, they can get a healthy perspective on themselves and develop a sense of humor and proper perspective about life, knowing they don't have to succeed at everything. That is a huge life skill! They can learn that the most important thing about activity, for the vast majority of us, is not winning, but the health benefit from "getting in the zone" or finding an individual form of exercise that will benefit them for a lifetime.

If we know our child is uncoordinated, we need to encourage and monitor his successes. Within a context of pointing out that everyone has strengths and weaknesses, we should highlight our kid's strengths and get excited about any progress in strong or weak areas. We should also note if our school has an unrealistic approach to physical education. Do they expect kids to perform to certain athletic standards that favor coordinated kids? That is unfortunate. We should have a talk with school personnel about more realistic goals for physical education and advocate for a system based on personal progress. If the system compares kids for grades, we should make sure our kids understand that grades are often not accurate measures of their capabilities or their personal progress.

Whatever our child's particular weaknesses, it is crucial for us to realize that the true weaknesses and obstacles in life are fear, discouragement, and giving up. Our kids might be clumsy, ADHD, handicapped, autistic, tone deaf, nearsighted, or any other host of identifiable differences. So what? There was a time when being left-handed was considered a disadvantage, and kids were made to feel abnormal or not as capable because they were left-handed. When are we going to get past highlighting kids' deficits?

There are a host of adults whose life stories would tell us that deficits do not define who they are or what they can do. Temple Grandin's life (a professor at Colorado State University) tells us that even autism is a trait with which a kid can flourish, if they are given an understanding of what they can do, and hope for where they can go, and what they can accomplish. David Neeleman's life (the founder of Jet Blue airlines) tells us that ADHD is a trait with which a kid can flourish, if someone provides the encouragement that they are capable and can accomplish important things. Dr. Hallowell's life (a graduate of Harvard Medical School) tells us that dyslexia is a trait with which a kid can succeed, if they are embraced and encouraged and made to feel that they can do great things—even things that take lots of reading, though they may never be good at reading. John Nash's life (subject of the movie *A Beautiful Mind*) demonstrates that even schizophrenia can't keep us from great accomplishments. This list could go on for pages and pages of all the people who have faced incredible challenges and succeeded. What is needed is support for our children's spirits, for their internal resilience and personal vision. When are we as adults going to stop predicting kids' futures by what they can't do? When are we going to start investing in every child based on what they can do?

Now you can see why my third idea in this chapter is so incredibly important. We need to give our kids a sense of what they can do, a positive vision for their future. This is an incredible opportunity for any parent in the life of their child. The greatest gifts we can give our children are our love for them and our belief in them. You can believe that even though they have deficits, that even though they fail, that even though they will face challenges, that even though they may be fearful and hesitant, they will go important places and do important things.

Oh, the Places You'll Go!

This mind-set in our children begins with us, and I wish I could say that we adults always support our kids. Often, however, our kids have to succeed in spite of adults.

I am thankful there are children in this world who don't pay attention to adults at times. I have read that Albert Einstein's parents were told by his Catholic school headmaster that he would never amount to much. This same message was later repeated to Albert by his Greek teacher. It is good for the world he didn't take these sentiments to heart. It is one thing to describe a negative situation accurately and seek a solution. "Your grade in Greek is a D. What can we do to improve that?" It is another thing to attribute causes. "You're failing Greek because you're lazy." It is yet another level of disservice to a child to predict failure in the future. "You're failing because you're a loser and will never amount to anything."

It is unbelievable that these kinds of statements are actually said to kids. When an adult makes such statements, what are they hoping to accomplish? Do we think this kind of talk motivates kids? These are the kinds of statements that make the situation worse. They can cause kids to stop trying and say, "What's the point?"

Kids are actually born with a desire to succeed. Every toddler continues to get up over and over again when they fall down. Every child at some point wants to please mom and dad and get their approval. Succeeding is built into kids!

In grade school, kids really do wish to learn. This is a natural human desire. Even kids who seem undisciplined and uncooperative love to learn. Let me say that again. Even kids who seem undisciplined and uncooperative love to learn! As a kindergarten teacher, my wife has experienced the following scenario over and over again. Every year she has children who for one reason or another cannot function appropriately in a classroom learning environment. They seem uncooperative and rebellious. Their problems may stem from an inability to pay attention, or behavior on the autistic spectrum, lack of parental discipline, or any number of other sources. As she proceeds through the year and learns more about the child, she will begin to work with "the team" to address the problem.

Her team includes parents, social workers, medical professionals, other teachers, her principal, and anyone who is appropriate to help create a solution. The amazing finding in child after child who can't function in the classroom is that once causes are understood and dealt with, the child is excited to learn and excited to function as a part of the classroom. This is true of the most unruly and undisciplined kids. This is true of kids who have given her bruises in the classroom. These kids, every one of them, want to learn and succeed.

Sometimes, the change in these kids is slow and comes in small steps, and sometimes it is almost overnight. She has had numerous children who have been recalcitrant, rebellious, and undisciplined in the classroom. They wouldn't follow or respond to instruction and appeared unwilling to cooperate. However, when an effective approach or medication was found, the child became cooperative and excited that they could function in the classroom. They were eager to learn and revealed that underneath their troubled behavior, they really wanted to cooperate and fit in. They simply didn't have the capability. They might have that Ferrari brain with the Model T brakes. Without help, they couldn't slow down or stop in order focus in the classroom.

I don't say this because my wife is an expert in this, but because she has witnessed year after year children who could have been written off as behavior problems. What they needed was not a prediction of failure, but an adult world willing to take the time and interest to understand, to work on solutions, and to provide support.

I love the story of Dr. Hallowell's first grade teacher.[18] Dr. Hallowell is a very successful psychiatrist and is someone who has dealt personally with ADHD and dyslexia throughout his life. He says he wouldn't trade away these traits of ADHD and dyslexia given the choice.

In first grade, he was blessed with Mrs. Eldridge. She had taught children, as he says, "for about 95 years" and understood them. Her reading program for kids with learning challenges consisted primarily of a supportive arm. Dr. Hallowell relates that as he was daily asked to demonstrate his obvious incompetency in reading, Mrs. Eldridge would come over beside him, place her arm around him, cradle him against her bosom, and provide support. Dr. Hallowell relates he would feel so safe. No one would dare laugh with Mrs. Eldridge right there.

He learned to like reading. Not because he was a magical story of a transformed reader who went from failing to succeeding, but because of how Mrs. Eldridge encouraged him. By the end of first grade he was the most enthusiastic, lousiest reader in the classroom. He became a six-year-old boy who looked forward to reading. And he never became a great reader. He spent a lot of time struggling through books as he graduated from Harvard in English while doing pre-med. Why would he do that?

He says it was Mrs. Eldridge who made him feel safe, who gave him constant encouragement, constant support, and a hope that he could read and that he could succeed. She helped him understand that he was talented and capable, that he would succeed at reading and life, and that he just had to work harder at reading than most other kids. She was absolutely right! Dr. Hallowell relates that she banished fear, embarrassment, and shame from his life, which, he says, were the real disabilities he faced.

Providing our children a vision of what they can become means, first of all, never writing them off. It means, to the best of our ability, believing in them and helping them understand that they can accomplish important things in our world. We can become even more effective in this by becoming a student of our children.

I originally learned the idea of becoming a student of our children from a guy named John Trent. He grew up without a dad but had huge respect for his mom. One of the things his mom did that really impressed me was she became a student of each of her kids. John relates that if you went to her home, you would find books and magazines on heavy construction and things like D9 Cats.[19] What is an older, single lady with no apparent interest in heavy construction doing reading magazines on earth-moving equipment?

The reason is simple: one of her sons makes his living in this industry. She made it a purposeful goal to try and understand her children, to become interested in what they were interested in, so that she could be a part of their lives and support them. She has learned about D9 Cats, because her son is into them. She has supported and encouraged his pursuit. She has done this with each of her kids, and you would find information in her house on each one of their professions. This is a great example for us. As a student of our children, we can help them understand themselves.

Our experience was roughly as follows. During the Filler years, we began helping our kids understand their basic temperament and the resulting strengths and weaknesses, which I have already discussed. During the Follower years, we continued this discussion on temperament and strengths and weaknesses, and added taking note of their interests and loves and worked to encourage growth in these areas. We also worked to expose them to a variety of opportunities.

This was not a revolutionary approach but looked more like supporting our kids in their musical, dance, or horseback riding interests, pointing out which subjects they seemed to like and do well in, encouraging them to try new things, and emphasizing that failure is the way we learn.

In their later Follower years and Finder years, we kept watching these things, but we also spent time envisioning and talking about their particular combination of traits and interests, and how those might serve them well in particular jobs or professions. Each of us should be looking at our children's abilities, interests, and traits with a goal both of understanding them and then helping them understand themselves. This understanding can then be used to help transmit a vision to our children for what they could become. This is one important way in which we help our Finders find out who they are. Once our kids catch a vision (though it may take years), they are much more likely to struggle through great obstacles to pursue that vision.

The Finder Years' Problem

The reality is that if we only begin this process in the Finder years, we may run into the fairly common problem that our kids have already stopped listening to us. This does present a significant challenge. It is difficult, if not impossible, to communicate a vision to a child who is no longer listening. I think in this situation especially, we need to have a team approach.

Let's turn to Dr. Robert Brooks for a story that might show how a team approach can help when we involve someone who understands the importance of having a vision for what our children can accomplish.[20]

After Dr. Brooks gave a seminar in dealing with angry kids, one of his seminar attendees returned to the high school where she worked to be given a seemingly impossible assignment. Her principal handed her the names of the five worst students and told her that since she had gone to this seminar, she had the job of correcting these kids' attendance and behavior problems. Her immediate reaction was to think she had been given an impossible task.

As Dr. Brooks relates the story, she thought about this impossible task and knew she was going to have to change, as the five kids weren't going to change. She called the kids in and met with them. She told them, "The Principal gave me a very important job yesterday. He is trying to understand why some kids do not want to go to school and why others do want to go to school. It's much too big a job for one person, and I need a committee of experts. I checked the records. You five may be the best we have."

One of the kids actually agreed, "We are!"

This could be a gimmick, but consider what she did. She then asked, "How are we going to study this?" So they developed a little questionnaire to find out two or three reasons a kid wants to go to school and two or three reasons a kid doesn't want to go to school.

She interviewed them and then told them, "We need more data." This then became a research study. She arranged for them to interview the superintendent of schools, the school board, teachers, principals, and other kids. They put together a report and presented it to the school committee. There were many recommendations.

One great recommendation that these kids made was that their ad hoc committee should become a standing committee meeting every day after school, because, as they noted, this problem of not wanting to go to school begins very early in a kid's life.

The school district made a change based on their recommendations, and during the day, every first grade teacher in the school district sent his or her attendance sheet to this committee. At the daily committee meeting, they then reviewed these attendance sheets to identify any first grader who had been out a certain number of days. When they identified a child, one of these five kids would personally go to visit that first grader to talk about the importance of going to school.

The school social worker wrote, "I know I am not always going to get results like this, but I love this strength-based approach, because in the three months since we started this, not one of these kids has been out one day, and we have not had one behavior problem."

These results were astounding. This social worker changed the lives of five of the worst kids in her high school. How did she do it? She found something they were good at—not going to school—and she treated it as a strength, and then asked how could they use their strength to give them a vision for something positive they could accomplish.

These five kids caught the vision, and it changed them.

I am reasonably sure that these five kids had stopped listening to their parents. But someone besides mom or dad caught their attention and communicated a vision. The strength was not something that most of us would recognize. Most parents would

continue to punish the kids for not going to school and try to change
their behavior, usually through negative means such as taking away
privileges and grounding, etc. The social worker, after listening to
Dr. Brooks, turned this problem on its head, and found a way to
make the problem itself a strength, and the kids responded.

This same thing can happen to our kids, as well, after they've
tuned us out, but it will likely take an interested adult (or even
another student) with a vision for what our kid can do. We have
to be careful with our intentions, though. Working with people
who are in influential positions around our children to give them a
vision is not the same thing as trying to control our kids through
others.

I often see parents attempting to control a child through others
after he has tuned them out. The conversation with our circle of
influence usually revolves around the question, "How can I get
them to...How can we keep them from..." and we fill in the blank
with what we think best. These approaches attempt to control
rather than support our kids' drive to become an adult. This is
a very different conversation than one that begins, "I want you to
be aware of some of the tremendous gifts and potential I see in my
child...."

The controlling conversation doesn't usually work with Finders
and essentially pushes them further away. If we know our child
and can help another person understand our child and see their
incredible value and potential, that other person may have a chance
to transmit a vision that may change our child's life.

We have to make a difficult choice when our child has rejected
us and our input as a parent. The natural focus is to try and restore

the relationship. The problem with this is that the Finder years are not about restoring the family focus of the Follower years, but about launching them into their life as adults. Progress requires great unselfishness in us as parents to pursue and support our child's need for growth into adulthood, rather than our need to restore the earlier parent-child relationship. Every interested parent hopes to be a significant part of their child's journey into adulthood, and there is every reason to believe we can play that part, but the reality is that sometimes this relationship breaks down.

If the relationship does break down totally, it is best for parents to do what they can to support their children's transition into adulthood. Working to help them find a vision through teachers, coaches, counselors, pastors, friends, etc., may be the most supportive approach parents can take. When my dad kicked me out of our house, he kicked me into a situation in which a vision was born. He did not transmit the vision, but acknowledged my independence and my need to work things out as an adult. He did not see my fighting with Mom as productive for any of us and stepped in to push me toward where my development was taking me anyway.

I went to live with my sister and brother-in-law, where I was no longer viewed as a child, but accepted as an equal and productive member of the family team and put to work. I was happy to play that role and learned a lot about family and relationships. This experience birthed attitudes and ambitions that could not have been birthed by staying at home.

To be clear, I am not recommending that you boot your cantankerous kid out at sixteen. What I am saying is that your work should be to launch the child into adulthood, and your attitude should be that this may not be an easy or appreciated job, especially if the child has essentially shut you out. The hope is that anything you do to affirm your kid's progress into adulthood and give them a vision will likely be the fastest way to an improved relationship.

In this process of helping our kids find a vision, there are a few things to keep in mind. First, any ideas we have regarding visions for our children need to be based on our knowledge of their abilities and interests, not what we want them to do. Some of us as parents have an extremely difficult time distinguishing what we wish our child would do and what are helpful choices for them based on who they are. Sometimes the test comes in the form of our kids choosing something we wish they wouldn't choose.

I am not talking about doing drugs or other dangerous activities, but something we have a difficult time envisioning for their sake and not ours. Maybe they want to join a rock and roll band, and we have other ambitions for them. Maybe they want to be an art history major, and we can't imagine how they will make a living in a tight economy. Maybe they have been pursuing a pre-med ambition and then become interested in a volunteering for charity work, and we don't think that is realistic. Maybe they've been helping in the family business and then they decide in high school they want nothing to do with it. Whatever it is, these decisions and how we react can help us understand whether we want them to truly become adults responsible for their own choices, or whether we are standing in the way of that process and trying to get them to fulfill our dreams.

This is a chance to see whether it is our vision and our priorities we are trying to pass on to our kids, or an honest release of them into adulthood, offering our support and approval to whatever extent they will receive it. Sometimes when the situation is full of conflict, it may be helpful to turn to others in order to get some honest input about whether we are trying to fulfill our dreams through our child, or whether we are releasing and supporting that child to become his or her own person.

A friend of mine struggled with a parent who would not release him to become his own person. Every meeting with that parent was filled with hints of his poor choices, and examples of what he could be doing, where he could be going. He heard comparison after comparison to others who were "making the right choices". The net effect of this was he simply distanced himself from both parents. Even then his choices were haunted by confusion. If he did the "right" thing, was he just caving into that parent? If he did the opposite, was that a way to scream I want to be free to determine who I am? Instead of being free, many of his choices were a reaction to that parent.

My friend wasn't a drug addict or a terrorist. He was a decent guy with his own ideas, successes, and failures. Instead of being prepared for adulthood, and then released and encouraged by his parents in his choices and pursuits, he spent most of his Finder and Fulfiller years fighting his parents and trying to break free of them. He did break free, but wasted a lot of time in the process.

What a difference it would have made for his parents to have essentially said the following: *You're an adult now. You will enjoy your good choices and learn from your lousy choices. These are all the good qualities we have seen in you, and we believe in you and love you. Here's*

how we will support you and work with you in the coming years if you are
open to that.

We will discuss some of the details of supporting our adult kids
in the Fulfiller chapter, but the message to take to heart here is that
the primary job of any parent, whether you are a duck, a monkey,
or a human, is to prepare their offspring for adulthood and then
release them to become an adult.

Let's review this situation and what I have said. The problem
is usually Finders who have checked out of trying in school
and stopped listening to their parents. They are motivated, but
it is a motivation to avoid a world that seems to them to bring
criticism, embarrassment, and failure. For whatever reason, they
have concluded that can't measure up, they can't succeed, and they
appear to have given up trying and caring.

What these kids need is a vision for what they can accomplish.
They need to gain a sense of their strengths and value. They need
a break from criticism and embarrassment, and an invitation to
succeed.

Parents may find they are suspicious of our attempts to
help them and consequently reject those attempts. We are still
responsible for them as parents and must continue our work to keep
them safe and set appropriate boundaries. Those limits for their
safety are most effectively presented and enforced in a framework
that acknowledges and works toward the goal of providing adult
freedom and responsibility.

Our efforts are likely most effective when we work with their
circle of influence by contacting teachers, relatives, church workers,
social workers, counselors, neighbors, and friends to see if anyone

we know is interested in our child's welfare and has his or her respect and attention. If we can find that person or group of people, we can help them understand what strengths we see in our young adult and admit our situation of having lost influence in his or her life. We must be careful not to apply pressure or have expectations that this person can solve the problem. We haven't done it, so why should we think they can? Simply be grateful that another adult is interested in our child, and then give them whatever information we can that might be helpful.

Many of us who caught a vision that motivated us after we had checked out and stopped listening to our parents, caught that vision with the help of another person (usually an adult) who we felt understood us and was interested in our welfare.

A Vision for the Finder Years – Summing It Up:

In summary, giving our kids a vision for what they can accomplish in life is possibly the most helpful thing we can do.

- In the best scenario, this vision is built over the Filler, Follower, and Finder years by helping our children understand their personalities, their strengths and weaknesses, and by implanting ideas about how their unique talents will create opportunities that could bring about significant accomplishments.

- In the most difficult situations, we may have to rely on someone else to help our kids see their incredible value. Any information about their strengths that we can provide to this other person or persons is helpful. Our goal in all of this is not to control them to do what we want, but to launch them into the adult world with a sense of what they can accomplish.

If our kids truly believe they have strengths and gain a vision for how they can use those strengths, they will likely endure great adversity, if necessary, to make progress toward goals consistent with their strengths. Remember that this takes time. Brain development takes years. We must exercise great patience as parents and never stop believing in our kids.

Chapter 9

Fulfiller

L ooking at an eighteen to twenty year old can be deceiving. Their shoe size is what it will be for the rest of their life, their hands won't grow any more, they've reached their full height, and they probably grow hair like an adult. That is what you can see. However, you can't see their brain.

Brain changes are still taking place. Yes, Fulfillers do have a nearly adult brain, and it's not going to significantly increase in density or size, but even now, it is not fully myelinated or fully online. Likely our eighteen year old is not the same person they will be when they are twenty-five. The evidence of these brain changes is that behavior and mental capabilities are still developing. We have said earlier that brain development continues into the mid-twenties as areas continue to come more fully online through myelination. This process of coming online increases the speed at which areas of the brain operate making them more efficient and effective.

Your eighteen year old is an adult, but more specifically from a brain perspective, they are a *developing* adult. They left childhood years ago and started the process of becoming an adult in earnest. The biggest mistake we can make at this stage is to assume that their brain and personality development is as complete as their physical growth. It is not.

Up until this chapter, we have focused on the major and obvious characteristics of the Filler, Follower, and Finder stages. We really haven't looked at the more subtle changes that are taking place during those phases. I hope you understand that a multitude of changes are taking place constantly through these stages, and for those of us interested, Neuroscience and Developmental Psychology can offer a more in-depth understanding of those changes. We now have an opportunity to look a bit more in-depth at some of the subtle changes that happen within a stage. We have a challenge, because this stage is the least researched of all the stages, however, some of the best information I have found comes from the MIT Young Adult Development Project.[21]

Growing out of adolescence takes simple abstract thinking (thinking abstractly about one thing) to more complex levels, allowing our kids to consider multiple abstractions and ways to organize those abstractions.

Adolescent thinking tends to see things as wrong or right, as black or white, largely missing any shades of grey. During the Fulfiller Stage, the continued brain development enables our kids to hold and appreciate multiple points of view. This means that appreciation for parental thinking may come back in vogue during this period.

I think many of us are familiar with a quote that has been attributed, possibly inaccurately, to Mark Twain, "When I was a boy of fourteen, my father was so ignorant I could hardly stand to have the old man around. But when I got to be twenty-one, I was astonished at how much he had learned in seven years." This is a great quote and reflects a significant part of what is different between the brains of a Finder (fourteen years old) and a Fulfiller (twenty-one years old).

At fourteen, children will tend to only hold one viewpoint that they perceive to be correct (black or white), and because of their oppositional tendencies, chances are that it will be different than their parents on many issues. By age twenty-one, brain changes allow their perspectives to broaden. Sometime, likely after age eighteen, they will think, *I have my ideas, but I can see value in my parent's ideas.* They may even come to appreciate ideas that they may have rejected earlier. There is a huge temptation for parents to say, "I told you so," or "The old man is not as dumb as you thought." We need to resist these temptations. If we have kept records of our disagreements and therefore tend to continue to make issues out of them, our kids will sense that. They are not coming back to us to get their noses rubbed in what we perceive to be their mistakes. If we do that, they will likely go elsewhere for adult wisdom and perspective.

Mark Twain's comment is entirely understandable. At age fourteen, he had an appropriate perspective considering his brain development. It's not that he was wrong and needed correction; it's that he was using his brain to the extent of its development. From a typical parental perspective, you could say he was not appreciative of his father's wisdom and was being a smart aleck. From a brain development perspective, he was learning for himself to become his own person and have his own ideas. These ideas in the Finder years tend to be framed in a totally right or totally wrong perspective.

Think of it this way. In walking, you held your child's hands and helped them along. They actually walked better by holding your hands than they did when they first wanted to do it on their own. They went from not walking, to walking across the room with your help, to trying to walk on their own and stumbling and falling down, to walking across the room on their own. And you loved it. This is a big oversimplification, but it helps our parental perspective. Your child is going from not thinking conceptually (Filler stage), to thinking with you "holding their hands" (Follower stage), to thinking on their own and struggling with this skill (Finder stage), to thinking very capably on their own (Fulfiller stage). Can you love this process as much as you loved watching them learn to walk? Keep in mind it takes a whole lot longer and is a whole lot messier.

The less we make the differences in our thinking and perspectives a battleground, the sooner our kids are likely to come to appreciate our perspective, as Mark Twain did his father's perspective. We as the parents will largely determine if this process becomes a battle or a time in which development is supported and encouraged. What makes the difference?

Here are some examples of the mistakes I made or was tempted to make throughout this process.

The first problem I had was that I tended to turn too many normal, but misunderstood, developmental characteristics into good or bad (if I took the moral perspective) or into disorders (if I took the medical perspective). If my child was being bad, he or she needed correction or punishment. If my child had a disorder, he or she needed an intervention. But if my child was developing, he or she simply needed appropriate support, patience, and encouragement.

If Mark Twain's fourteen-year-old attitude had been known by his dad he could have been a) punished from a moral perspective (*Show some respect*), b) sent to a counselor from a disorder perspective (*Something is wrong with you, and it needs to be fixed*), or c) accepted and encouraged from a developmental perspective (*Hey, you're thinking on your own! Fantastic! That may lead to some disagreements between us, but it is good to see*). I think c) is the correct response for most issues and ought to be our default response.

There are times in which our kids know what we expect from them, have the capability to do it, and knowingly choose not to do it. That deserves corrective action. There are some situations in which development is not progressing along a usual continuum. That needs an intervention. But both of these should be the exceptions in our response.

A second problem I had was that I took normal developmental responses in my child too personally. At some point, my fourteen year old may have thought I was stupid. If I didn't take this as a developmental stumble in their thinking, and instead got offended, this drew battle lines very quickly. It was very easy to listen to the words apart from the context and conclude, "This child has stepped over the line," and engage the comment head-on about being stupid. A much better reaction would be to let the comment

roll off you in the moment, try and get down to the real need, and
tackle his or her choice of words later when moods are better.

Even tackling the choice of words should not be, "You're wrong,"
but rather "Calling me stupid does not help us work through the
issue." Another way to answer the stupid comment by your young
adult might be, "Hey, there are better ways to express yourself, but
thanks for trying. It helps me know what is going on inside so that
we can work on it. Please use 'I feel you're being stupid' or 'That
doesn't seem smart' as better choices of words."

The third problem I faced was the temptation to give in to social
pressure related to child rearing. For many us, this often takes the
form of thinking our kids shouldn't have problems and attempting
to display how wonderful, normal, advanced, and creative our kids
are. It is great to be proud of our kids, but sometimes we are saying,
I'm okay and I've done a great parental job, because my kid is so great. Ouch!
This does not let kids be works in progress. If I'm embarrassed by
the mess-ups my kids have made or by the developmental challenges
they face, I need to adjust my attitude. The world has too many
kids who feel they could never live up to their parents' expectations.
This is an attitude handicap that can be worse than developmental
problems themselves and is completely avoidable.

As a kid, I stuttered like crazy. My parents were great. They
never made excuses, tried to correct, or in any way brought attention
to it. They got me a speech therapist in middle school to help, but
I don't ever remember my stammering affecting them at all. They
accepted it as a part of the total package they loved.

I'm sure there are other mistakes I made as well, but we need to
keep in mind this quote by Mark Twain. He did come to appreciate

what his dad knew. His development followed a normal process, and he went from mental stumbling at age fourteen to a broader mental perspective at age twenty-one. Our kids will follow this process successfully as well, especially if we accept, engage, support, and encourage their thoughts and individual perspectives rather than fighting with them.

When our kids become Fulfillers and become capable of more complex perspectives, we simply need to welcome the change. If we consider the ideas that they held in high school to be inadequate and in need of our correction, we have the wrong perspective. This would be the same as holding any other normal developmental inadequacy against them: whether it is spitting out their food as an infant, stumbling as a toddler, or not being able to grasp relationship complexities as a grade-schooler. What would the point of that be? We wouldn't do this over any of these things because we have the right perspective.

In all of these instances our children are learning and not being compared with us or in competition with us. In the same way, highlighting the limitations of adolescent thinking (Teen Think) is pointless. What we are witnessing is the wonderful process of how brains develop. Don't miss the beauty of this.

Another situation we may find ourselves in as our kids grow into adults is unrealistic memories. You may find that your son or daughter holds some surprising views of what happened in their lives. The most threatening kind of memories for us as parents are those in which our children think we failed them. Our daughter may burst into tears at some point and accuse us of neglecting her in middle school, causing her to cry herself to sleep every night, or to hang out with destructive friends, or whatever other negative situation might have happened. Depending on the accusation, we might burst into tears and defend back. This creates a fight. It is best to pause before we respond to surprising revelations like this.

If the adolescent brain was not capable of complex thinking, or thinking in shades of grey, it would be very understandable that kids would not see a situation in its complexity. During middle school, one of their parents might have experienced unemployment, dad might have had an affair, or their parents might have gotten divorced. These things are difficult to understand for the best of us. It should not surprise us if our children conclude that we neglected them or failed them in some way, and they don't appreciate how hard we worked in their behalf.

It is best to understand that although this is not accurate, it is reality as they perceived it, and to admit that those were tough times and that we hope to continue to improve as parents. In actuality, this conversation often begins a phase in which our kids, as their brains become more capable, will come to a better appreciation of the difficulties we faced. Some of that understanding will only happen when they face similar situations. It is difficult for the brain in development to grasp all of the dimensions that difficult and complex situations involve. Although some of our kids can have incredible insight, a normal and developmentally appropriate Teen Think experience for them has a simplistic, black and white perspective of events that can lead them to different conclusions than ours.

We should allow children their perspective and look for opportunities to add to it over the years as their ability to discuss these issues increases. Likely they will come to better understand our difficult times, and the efforts we made over time. Let's not force them into an argumentative corner in which we accuse them of holding a wrong perspective. Their perspective may have been the best they could do at the time. Holding their own unique perspective is an accomplishment for them and part of their particular brain development. We have to work not to be threatened by their perspectives and conclusions.

In our own case, as we have listened to and accepted our kids' perspectives and loved them no matter what those perspectives are, we have found them open to talking about their perspectives and the ways in which we differ. This has brought natural opportunities to add more information to their thinking without seeking to change their minds. The result in our family has been very positive.

This is a good time to remember our job. We are first parents— not critics, teachers, ministers, or counselors. At times, we may do all of those things, but only after we fulfill our parental job. As parents, we are supporting and in devoted love preparing our kids for adulthood.

Let's review an example of what a difference this makes. Let's say your Finder child has just told you you're stupid and stomped down the hall and slammed his or her door. If we were critics first, we would describe how inappropriate this behavior is for getting the results we want. Teachers? We might point out the proper steps of engaging a disagreement. Ministers? We might remind them of the respect that is due to parents. Counselors? We might repeat their emotional words and attempt to provide insight into their emotional state to deal with it better. As parents, we would first affirm and embrace their development and perspective, and above all communicate that we love them and are committed to supporting their growth into adulthood no matter what comes in life. After working to communicate that, we would look for appropriate opportunities to give helpful input and any correction needed.

Our Finder and Fulfiller children may try to give input to us as parents. In fact, the time may come in which they wish to initiate conversation with us about significant life issues. In my early twenties, I once gave my mom a self-help book. From my perspective at that time, I thought she needed it. The problem was I got zero response. I could have been totally wrong in my estimation, but there was no way to know. The fact that my mom didn't say anything at all about the book meant we never talked. What a missed opportunity as a parent to have a conversation with your kid! If your child gives you a book, take the book and read it. Tell your kid you read the book and would love to have coffee over it. Discuss it. Be ready, because they might unload anything from advice for you to pent-up hostility. In the end, I bet there would be learning all the way around and an improved relationship. In my case, there was no discussion and that meant no relationship improvement.

Remember in this conversation that the more Finder characteristics they have, the more likely that they will be adamant that their position is right. The more Fulfiller characteristics they have, the more likely they will be to listen to alternative perspectives. We should be prepared to be good listeners and respond, keeping in mind that they may not be ready to hear our perspective. No need to argue. The need is to listen and comment, allowing them their perspective.

The Fulfiller years will likely bring another nice surprise. Because our children are getting better at holding multiple perspectives, this means they can begin to appreciate constructive criticism. Have you ever had a confrontation in which the climax was a strained or screamed, "Can't you understand I'm just trying to help you?" The ability to appreciate that another person is being helpful in a confrontation, though it feels painful, takes a certain amount of brain development.

As a Finder, a mature child may come back later and say they understand, but it will likely be because they have processed the events in a linear fashion over time. In other words, over time they figured out first, that dad was mad because I screwed up; second, dad wants me to be safe; third, dad gave me a speech because he wanted me to understand how I need to behave to stay safe; and fourth, it was probably not the best idea for me to stomp out of the room and slam the door. For these to all be held in the brain and processed at one time, with the understanding that dad was acting in their best interest is difficult for anyone, and probably not an ability most Finders have.

This will likely change in the Fulfiller years. Because kids are now better at keeping multiple perspectives in mind at the same time, they are better able to say to themselves, "This is painful, but they want the best for me, and I should listen."

We should not be surprised that it is difficult for our kids to recognize in the moment that confrontation may be in their best interest. Do we need to have these conversations? Absolutely. Do we need to drop the expectation that our kids will understand these conversations are in their best interest? Yes, as well. As I have said, the nice thing is that during the Fulfiller years, we may be pleasantly surprised that our kids will become better at understanding that a confrontation can be helpful and in their best interest.

The Fulfiller years may bring still another pleasant surprise. It is common for adolescents, especially boys, to have no idea what they want to do with their lives. They appear to us at times as passionless blobs, filling space and time, going nowhere. One reason this can happen, especially to boys, is slow emotional development. I have often seen this in Finder boys.

As I have said earlier, this can be made worse when we as parents make our kids' decisions for them or save them from the consequences of their decisions. Either one of these means our kids really don't get decision-making practice and don't develop their decision-making ability. The nice thing is that, hopefully in the Fulfiller years, circumstances force our kids to get practice making decisions, and emotions naturally mature.

Remember that emotions help us to make decisions and to be passionate about life. It is common for a Finder boy to be slower in emotional development than his female counterpart, and when asked what he wants to do with his life, he will often say, "I don't know." Part of the reason for this is likely the slower maturation of the frontal cortex and its primary decision-making aid, the emotional area of his brain. He really doesn't know what he wants. He doesn't feel passionate about anything.

The Fulfiller years will bring more maturing and more effective and efficient connections between the frontal cortex and

the emotional areas of the brain, and you will see your son begin
to have opinions, to feel passionate about certain things, to begin
to be more decisive. It is very important to keep in mind that a
passive and disengaged son may simply need time for his brain to
develop more. It is very common for boys (and even men at times)
not to know how they feel. (Remember that we are talking about
general trends. It is also very possible to have a finder boy that is
very passionate about things, or have a finder girl who doesn't know
what she wants. All brains are different and vary to one extent or
another.)

If our kids cannot seem to make decisions, we as parents need to
utilize other areas of their brains. Instead of asking them how they
feel about possible careers or what major they want to study, explain
to them their need to make some choices in this area. Usually a
kid will be fairly responsive to a well-explained need. Choosing a
college major is a good example. Because we as parents are putting
out piles of cash to educate our kids, it can be rather disconcerting
to have a child who continually says, "I don't know," when you ask
about their major. In our case, when that came up, we explained to
our child that the way to figure out your opinion about something
is to choose a direction and start heading there.

"It's like a ship," we explained. "If it's not moving, you can't
direct it no matter how much you turn the rudder." In the same
way, some kids can sit and think about something like a major and
find that they have no opinion. It is best in that situation to simply
pick one, because as they start moving in a certain direction, they
will find that the experience of that particular choice helps them
form an opinion about it, even if all they learn is that they should

head another direction. Their interaction with classes, professors, and other students in a particular major will assist them in forming these feelings and opinions. In the beginning of this process, they may simply be eliminating majors or jobs they don't like. That's okay. It is better for them to have headed down the education or career path and eliminated five majors or jobs they don't like, than to still be sitting at the dock, not knowing anything more about what they do and don't like.

In this case, then, I am not recommending that you let your children wait for an underdeveloped emotional connection to mature before making any life choices. I am presenting an approach that made sense to our kids: defining their job as choosing any specific path, looking to find whether they liked it or not. They will likely say, "I can't decide," if their emotional system is not mature. Tell them it doesn't matter; if they continue heading in a certain direction long enough, how they feel about that direction will become clearer. As they grow into the Fulfiller years, and their frontal cortex and emotional areas mature and become better connected, they will begin to be passionate about certain things, and decisions will become easier.

This means as parents we must let our kids change their minds and not get exasperated. This is decision-making practice. As I continue to say, the earlier we allow them to make decisions of consequence, the better. Unfortunately, I meet a lot of Fulfillers that are just getting started making decisions of consequence for themselves, because mom and dad have made their decisions for them.

What are some signs that progress is not going normally in the Fulfiller state? Continuing depression would be one sign. Even when my kids haven't had a clue about what direction they should head for regarding a major or a career, they still had energy and interest in activities, friends, learning, and having fun. If those disappear, and a lingering cloud of despair descends for extended periods of time, it probably is reasonable to head for a counselor.

What are other signs that a counselor is needed? In general, when we see progress stall or go backwards over time (Teen Think is the exception). Every kid is concerned about their appearance to some extent or another. Problems arise when they get stuck on that theme over time, and dieting becomes a more and more serious endeavor. Every kid can tend to be oppositional. Problems arise when that oppositional tendency does not begin to resolve itself over a period of years. Every kid can tend to be compulsive about certain things. Problems arise when kids are compulsive to an unusual extent and can't get their hands clean, for example. Every kid gets anxious and can't sleep. Problems arise when anxiety rules their mind, and the sleeplessness becomes chronic.

Even though we are not dealing specifically with developmental problems in this book, I think it is important to keep loose tabs on how are kids are doing mentally, even if they are away at school. Their brains are still in a developmental stage, and things can go wrong. In our case, we have managed to keep fairly open lines of communication with our kids at college, and we provide help and advice when appropriate. We might need to encourage them to set up a doctor's appointment, or help them understand that chronic sleeplessness is not good, even if they have a lot of homework. As parents, we have lived with them for years and should have a fairly good sense of when they are doing well and when they are having trouble. Their roommates and friends at college are not necessarily going to know what is normal for them and what is not. All of this needs to happen in the context of us treating them and respecting them as capable, self-determining adults.

As adults they may not want or accept this kind of help from us. If that is the case, the best approach is to respect their adult choices and not intrude. This may be the only path to building trust between us. They need to know that we respect their wishes, decisions, and independence as adults. Once they are secure in that understanding, they may be more open to share their lives with us.

Tracking Stress

It is important to remember that chronic stress is one of the deterrents to healthy brain development at any age. There are plenty of things that can stress our kids in this stage. They're working on relationships, figuring out specifically what they want to do with their life, and trying to learn out what it means to live as an adult in a rapidly changing society. They are bombarded with media hype, and constantly tempted to burn the candle at both ends. All of our technological advances have not necessarily improved our quality of life. What they have done is increase the speed at which life comes at us.

For this reason, I sense it is more difficult to navigate the transition into adulthood than when I was a young adult, and the possibility for our kids to experience unhealthy levels of stress has increased. My experience suggests that many parents add to this level of stress rather than reduce it. Three of the ways we do this are through conflict, uncertainty, and hovering.

I have already mentioned conflict in this chapter. It can be subtle or overt conflict. Subtle conflict can come from parents not quite approving of our kids' choices. Conflict comes when we challenge their choices and even their right to make those choices. We maintain expectations of what they should do and become, and when they don't comply, we either withhold approval or get in their face.

My parents created conflict with me by offering help that I really could have used, but only if I did things their way. Fortunately, I had a sense as a young adult that self-determination of my life was more important than parental help with strings attached. I knew I would have to live the rest of my life with the choices I made. They wouldn't have to.

One example was when my mom offered financial help if I would attend one of the colleges she approved. I felt the choice was very clear: allowing them to help me financially meant I adopted Mom as a majority partner into my adult life. I viewed this as a decision not to leave home and remain a child. I had absolutely no problem and did not hesitate with this decision. I rejected the help. I knew that whatever my life would become as an adult, it had to follow a path that I chose, not a path that was chosen for me. Fortunately, my mom did not challenge my rejection of her offer, and my dad ensured that my choices were respected. I also did not waste time worrying about pleasing my mom and dad. I would respect and honor them as parents, but I would not invite them to live my life for me.

It is very important for our Fulfiller children to see themselves as self-determining adults. It becomes critical when we marry. It is damaging to a newly formed relationship between a husband and wife if one of them has never left home. There are enough challenges in working out a new life between two people without having a third party (parents) integrally involved.

My parents could have chosen to disapprove of my choices. This would have been a continuing source of stress. I saw this struggle in friends of mine whose parents would not let go of the unfulfilled expectations they had for their kids.

These expectations can have to do with the career kids choose, the company they keep, or the lifestyle they adopt. Parents can voice their disapproval directly or they can drop hints in tones of disappointment, in comparisons with others who are making the "right" choices, or in withdrawing and giving the silent treatment for choices we make. As parents, we need to get over the disappointment and stop these harmful tactics.

It is time to let go of expectations, get out of our kids' way, and offer to encourage them in their adult journey. We encourage them through accepting and supporting them in their choices. We support their choices by being a part of their team and larger community network.

This support brings me to the second point of uncertainty. I think as parents we need to be concrete about what we will do and won't do as part of their support network. I have witnessed parents offering financial help to kids but never saying how much help, or for what, or when.

"Just let us know when you need money" can become a source of uncertainty. What does "need money" mean? Kids can suggest, "I need money for a dance class." Parents might reply, "Well, that's not a real need, sweetie. Let us know when you have a real need."

It is so much better to let your kids know how much support you are able to give them, when you can give it, and then follow your plan and commitment to them. If they are to be adults who plan ahead and make choices and deal with the consequences of those choices, we can't be withholding financial support every time we don't agree with their choices.

An example of a good plan is to state how much support you will give them if they choose to go to college or a trade school. For example, "We have been saving in a college fund and we are able to pay tuition at a state school for the next four years. You will have to come up with room and board and any other spending money you wish to have. You are welcome to live at home and go to a local school. If you choose to go to a private school or out of state school, we can give you $9,000 each year toward your tuition bill. To us, what going to school means is conducting yourself in such a way that you will be able to graduate in four to five years. This means following a plan to get a degree, and we do not consider flunking classes going to school."

What we are saying to our children is that if college is their choice in pursuing their adult life, we will support them in a specific way. Now, a kid knows how to plan. If she chooses to go to school, it is now clear that up to $9,000 will be provided for tuition if she works to pass her courses in pursuit of a degree. When we do this, we should not be trying to control our children or their decisions, but simply stating how much and how long we will support them in their final transition to adulthood.

I grew up in a religious family and have been involved in religious circles my entire life. Often religious parents have a very tough time understanding this principle. There is a story from the Bible that I think speaks to the religious and non-religious alike. It is the story of the prodigal son found in the book of Luke, chapter 15.

It is a story in which the youngest child in a family decides he wants to leave the family and the family business and go to the big city. I don't think it was any secret that the kid intended to have a wild time. He approached his father about getting his inheritance early so he could fund this decision. Amazingly enough, the father gives him his inheritance.

As one might predict, he goes to the city and spends the money on a wild lifestyle and ends up broke. He then reflects on his choices and in the end returns home to a father who accepts him with love and open arms and even celebrates his return. I like this story and its point.

The father gave the son a bunch of money, knowing what was likely to happen. It would be common for many of us to say, "I'm not going to support this choice. When you make the right decisions, you can have your money." At this point, we would be attempting to keep our son a child and take from him his self-determination. This suggests our love and commitment to our son is conditional. "You do what we think you ought to do, and we will support you."

In the story, the father does not take this approach. He allows the son to take the resources he has committed to him and make his own choices. He allows him to be a self-determining adult, and it does not go well. However, what he gains in the end is that his son learns what his choices lead to and makes better choices. In this story, the father gets his son back as a self-determining adult. Their relationship is clearly based on free choices, not coercion.

This is an ancient story, but has continuing application to the Fulfiller years. This story, as many stories do, has a happy ending. In life, even the right choices do not always have happy endings. However, it is crippling to a young adult for parents to use their influence to keep them a dependent child.

One mild version of this I have also witnessed is hovering. This is when parents continue to push themselves into their kid's affairs through the excuse of kindness. Helping with this, giving opinions on that, rescuing when there are problems, and generally continuing their parental job of guiding and helping make decisions, often in a very kind and cheerful way. This is an insidious way of being so kind and helpful that your child never wants to grow up and take full responsibility for themselves and their decisions. In effect, you make them dependent through kindness. This is a bad choice as well.

The point is that we should have been preparing our Fulfillers to be self-determining adults for years. We should have begun to set them free in the Finder years, and that freedom should now be completed sometime in the Fulfiller years. We need to stop being a source of conflict and stress for our kids through attempts to control them and set them free to be the adults their bodies and brains are pushing them to be.

Fulfiller – Summing It Up:

Setting our kids free to be adults is the main focus of the Fulfiller years. This process begins in earnest in the Finder years. In this chapter we have seen that the Fulfiller years will likely bring the following changes.

- Brain development will bring an increasing capacity for complex thinking
  - o Our young adults will likely begin to see value in our opinions if they haven't before.
  - o They will begin to think more in shades of grey about issues rather than having a black and white perspective.
  - o They may be able to understand constructive criticism.
- Emotional development will progress in those who seem passionless. This will increase their desire and ability to become good decision makers.

Finally we discussed how we can reduce stress in our Fulfiller's lives by being clear and straightforward about the help that we intend to give them in their transition to adulthood. It is also critical to completely release them to be the adults they wish to become.

Chapter 10

Parenting Fulfillment

As I write this final chapter, my son is home from college for the weekend doing homework in the living room. My high school senior daughter is sleeping late, enjoying her last holiday before graduation. My other daughter is away at school, and I have no idea what she is up to at this precise moment. This time of life seems to my wife and me to be a good and healthy transition in which the control of their lives is being placed fully into their own hands. It seems good and healthy, because we find ourselves cooperating with what is going on developmentally in their brains.

In a very healthy way, they want to go out and make their own way in life. This is where cooperating with brain development should bring us in our parenting journey. Understanding healthy brain development has given us a road map for the journey we embarked on when we decided to have children.

The brain development characteristics of the Filler years made it clear that our children needed us to be close and involved. In fact, we became their very world, and their lives revolved around us. Their brains were uniquely designed to download our speaking, attitudes, and actions. Just as we gave them physical life through the interaction of sex, we give them the basis of their behavior and thought life through our social interaction with them.

Then brain development motivated them to branch out and want to explore, not away from us, but with us in the Follower years. The children tended to follow us, and we led them into new experiences. They were now active participants in their learning about life and began to draw more and more from events and people outside of their parents.

The Follower characteristics then provided us an opportunity to teach them about life and what we thought would be helpful for them to know. The entire time, they were still downloading from us and noting how well our lives went based on the decisions we made. This was the time of life to discuss all of the important topics of life and, in my opinion, the earlier the better.

One example of these important topics was talking to our kids about sex and understanding this is a conversation that begins very early in life and should take place over the Follower years rather than in one middle school talk. I have had numerous discussions with parents about "the talk." One of the interesting situations is when parents do "the talk" in a group way with a Follower and a Finder as listeners. Some parents have experienced the Finder acting like he or she is thinking, "When can we get this talk over?" while the Follower listens, asks some questions, and thinks about it. This response is an example of the different stages of their brain development and the varying opportunities of those developmental stages. The Follower years provide a fantastic opportunity to talk about everything of importance and to transmit our values and ideas on those subjects.

The Follower years are also a great time to let our kids make choices and decisions that have real consequences. These choices become learning opportunities for them on how to become better decision makers. The nice thing is that starting this decision-making practice in the Follower years means the consequences of lousy decisions are much less severe than later in life.

If we keep in mind that mistakes are the means by which we all learn, we can actually have a positive attitude toward their failing attempts at decision making. We can tell them that we all learn by failure and give them examples of how we have learned through failure. They need to know that this is the normal learning process and that failure is valuable. With practice, they will get better, and what an advantage it is to have your kids become Finders having had good decision making practice.

Next come the Finder years. They have a natural motivation through developmental changes in their brain to push away from us, to adopt different values and ideas, and to become their own person. Our understanding of brain development and its influence on how we worked with our kids in this stage was extremely helpful in minimizing conflict and misunderstanding. Trust me, all of that still existed, but we expected it and embraced it as having a good purpose. We did not view conflict as inherently destructive to our family but an expected step in our family's development.

We had relatively few sleepless nights and relatively few worries. Please note the word *relatively*, because we did have both. However, we had already accepted that our kids would make mistakes, and we would deal with them as adults as they happened. We had given our kids lots of decision-making opportunities and when we set them free around age sixteen, we experienced anxiety, but stuck to our plan. We accepted that life does not come with any guarantees, and that good or bad might happen as a result of their choices. We relaxed as parents, knowing we were cooperating with their appropriate developmental needs.

This is an important perspective to keep in mind. The issue is not whether you are going to be able to keep your children 100 percent safe. No matter what you do and how you approach this time of life, there are no guarantees. It is better to focus on what is developmentally appropriate than to have the unrealistic goal of making sure nothing bad ever happens.

That made a huge difference in our kids' teenage years, and they have communicated their appreciation to us many times. We wanted them to be adults. As a family, we value that we live in a country that champions personal liberty and the right to self-determination. This reflects a human desire that stems from how brains develop in a free society such as ours.

During these Finder years, we continued our work to give them a vision for their unique skills and strengths and the sense that they could be confident in making their own way in life. We also accepted that they had brains under construction that would not work well at times. As they stumbled learning to walk (demonstrating healthy motor development through mistakes) and we would cheer, so we tried to cheer as they slammed doors and gave us the silent treatment (demonstrating healthy emotional development through mistakes).

There are so many transitions that take place in the Finder years. As our kids became more and more independent, we offered ourselves as a permanent part of their supportive community as they moved into adulthood. Over time, we relinquished any control we might have in order to set them free. We have now seen them freely embrace us in their support network to one extent or another and in general more than we expected.

As I mentioned earlier in the book, we are now in the Fulfiller years, and this story is still being written. Happily, these kids that we have set free view their parents as a valuable resource in their lives now. We remind them that we are facilitating their continuing growth into adulthood, and there are limits to how much we can help. I think they get it and are looking forward to their futures.

I don't know what more we could ask for.

About the Author

Rick Doughty is a parent of three college-age children and works for the Oregon Health & Science University in Beaverton, Oregon. His wife Sally is a kindergarten teacher in the Beaverton School District. Rick is a Certified Trainer in brain-based education through the Jenson Learning Corporation and has a master's degree in communication studies. His passion is helping to make complex material and ideas useful and understandable

In keeping with this passion, Rick also presents Filler to Fulfiller Parenting as a speaker. This material can be presented in one overview session or multiple sessions to cover the particular stages more in depth.

For more information about this book, Filler to Fulfiller Parenting Seminars, or to contact Rick, visit him on his website at ftfparenting.com.

(Endnotes)

[1] Jensen, E. (2003). *Tools for engagement*. San Diego: Brain Store Inc.

[2] Senghas, A., & Coppola, M. (2001). Children creating language: How nicaraguan sign language acquired a spatial grammar. Psychological Science, 12, 323-328.

[3] Hibbeln, J. R. (1998). Fish consumption and major depression. Lancet, 351, 1213.

[4] Fletcher, R. H., & Fairfield, K. M. (2002). Vitamins for chronic disease prevention in adults: Clinical applications. JAMA, 287, 3127-3129.

[5] Christakis, D. A., Zimmerman, F. J., DiGiuseppe, D. L., & McCarty, C. A. (2004). Early television exposure and subsequent attentional problems in children. Pedatrics, 113, 708-713.

[6] Kuhl, P. K., Tsao, F. M., & Liu, H. M. (2003). Foreign-language experience in infancy: Effects of short-term exposure and social interaction on phonetic learning. Proceedings of the National Academy of Sciences of the United States of America, 100, 9096-9101.

[7] Macri, S., & Wurbel, H. (2006). Developmental plasticity of HPA and fear responses in rats: A critical review of the maternal mediation hypothesis. Hormones and Behavior, 50, 667-680.]

[8] Cirulli, F., Francia, N., Berry, A., Aloe, L., Alleva, E., & Suomi, S. J. (2009). Early life stress as a risk factor for mental health: Role of neurotrophins from rodents to non-human primates. Neuroscience and Biobehavioral Reviews, 33, 573-585.

[9] Sapolsky, R. (2005). Biology and Human Behavior: The neurological origins of individuality, Lecture four: Learning and synaptic plasticity. (2nd ed.) [DVD]. Available from http://www.thegreatcourses.com/tgc/courses/course_detail. aspx?cid=1597

[10] Jensen, E. (2006). Enriching the brain: How to maximize every learner's potential. San Francisco: Jossey-Bass Education.

[11] Amen, D., & Payne. J. (2005). Making a good brain great: Facilitator's guide. NewPort Beach: Mindworks, 2:9-10.

[12] Ibid, 8:17.

[13] Damasio, A. (1994). Descartes' error: Emotion, reason, and the human brain. New York: Grosset/Putnam.

[14] Seuss, D. (1990). Oh, the places you'll go! New York: Random House.

[15] Smally, G., & Trent, J. (1992). Session 1: Discovering personality strengths. [VHS]. No longer available. Homes of Honor Video Series.

[16] Smally, G., & Trent, J. (1992). Homes of honor manual. (Publication 9). Branson: Homes of Honor Publications, 9.

[17] Hallowell, E. (2008, November). Super-teaching and super-parenting for ADHD. Session presentation at the Learning and the Brain Conference: Using Emotions research to enhance learning. Cambridge, MA.

[18] Ibid.

[19] Smally, G., & Trent, J. (1992). Session 5: The Blessing. [VHS]. No longer available. Homes of Honor Video Series.

[20] Brooks, R. (2010 February). Mindsets for School Success: Nurturing effective educators and resilient, motivated learners. Session presentation at the 22nd Learning and the Brain Conference: using social brain research to enhance learning. San Francisco, CA.

[21] Simpson, A. R. (2008). Young adult development project. Retrieved from Young adult development project website: http://hrweb.mit.edu/worklife/youngadult/